Speed, Agility and Quickness

for

RUGBY

SAQ Rugby

Alan Pearson

A & C Black • London

Metric to Imperial conversions

1 centimetre (cm)	=	0.394 in
1 metre (m)	=	1.094 yd
1 kilometre (km)	=	1 093.6 yd
1 kilogram (kg)	=	2.205 lb

Reprinted 2006
First published 2001 by
A & C Black (Publishers) Ltd
38 Soho Square, London W1D 3HB

Copyright © 2001 by SAQ International Ltd

ISBN-10: 0 7136 5949 1
ISBN-13: 978 0 7136 5949 8

Alan Pearson has asserted his right under the Copyright, Design and Patents Act, 1988 to be identified as the author of this work.

A CIP catalogue record for this book is available from the British Library.

Throughout the book, players are referred to individually as 'he'. This should, of course, be taken to mean 'he' or 'she' where appropriate.

Acknowledgements

Cover photograph courtesy of Allsport; all other photographs courtesy of Pam Marshall; illustrations on pp. 137–9 by Dave Saunders. All other illustrations courtesy of angus Nicol and Carol Moore.

Typeset in Photina
Printed and bound in Great Britain by Biddles Ltd, Kings Lynn, Norfolk

Contents

Acknowledgements

A special thank you to Pam Marshall, Mike Penniston and the players of Nottingham Rugby Football Club. To Angus, Sarah, David and all those involved with SAQ INTERNATIONAL, thanks for all your hard work.

A very special thank you to Bob Dwyer, Dave Reddin, Dai Young, Dr Liam Hennessy, Mark Spivey and Iain Balshaw for their advice, support and belief in the SAQ Rugby Programme. Last but not least, all my love to my wonderful wife, Silvana for her caring support and understanding.

Alan Pearson
August 2001

Forewords

Throughout my coaching career, I've always tried to keep an open mind regarding anything that could positively influence my players or my coaching. This causes a bit of lost time chasing along a few dead ends, but that's the way I'm made.

With this mindset, I immediately accepted an approach from Alan Pearson when he offered to explain and demonstrate the benefits of the SAQ Programme. Happily this path was to prove anything but a dead end. I would go as far as to say that the SAQ Programme is the most influential performance-enhancing tool that I have seen in the last five years.

Without a doubt, it has become extremely difficult, if not impossible, for a player to reach the professional level without genuine leg speed. The SAQ Programme enables the player to achieve substantial gains in leg speed and power – horizontally, vertically and laterally – in the space of one off-season. I introduced the SAQ Programme on a trial basis during the 1996 season at Leicester Tigers RFC and it soon became obvious that the players were benefiting both physically and psychologically.

Continued use of the SAQ Programme can transform a 'player' into an 'athlete' – a player with much improved balance, agility and acceleration. In short, the kind of player we are all looking for. How wonderful then that we can now take our gifted 'players' and help them achieve the additional status of gifted 'athletes'.

In rugby, there continues to be debate about the so-called 'gulf' between the northern and southern hemispheres. In one area though, there can be no debate. The presence of the SAQ Programme, with its accompanying qualified SAQ Trainers puts the northern hemisphere, or at least the UK, a long way in front.

It was a good day for me, my career, and, hopefully my players when I was introduced to this simple, sensible, and enjoyable programme.

Bob Dwyer
Currently Director of Rugby for NSW Waratahs
World Cup Winning Coach, Australia (1991)
Director of Rugby, Leicester Tigers (1998)

We have used SAQ Training and SAQ Equipment since 1996, as a core part of our programmes to develop the speed and agility of our players. The concepts and drills of the SAQ Programme are scientifically based, practically researched and easily adaptable to different sports. Above all, the players enjoy them, which makes their effectiveness even greater.

Alan Pearson has always had an eye for fresh and different ideas, and I constantly pick up new drills and methods from talking to him. It is great to see this new book, which compiles so many of the tried and tested methods used with our players and many other club sides. I have no hesitation in recommending it to anyone interested in improving the performance of their players – whether at amateur, professional or international level.

Try it ... it works! And I guarantee that you will enjoy it.

Dave Reddin
National Fitness Adviser
England Rugby

Previously it was believed that qualities such as speed, agility and quickness could not be improved by training. SAQ Practitioners have, however, been developing these key skills in players and athletes for some years now.

SAQ Training methods provide the opportunity for exploiting a player's movement potential and also offer a structured programme for the development of basic motor skills in children, young athletes and players of all ages and abilities.

From my experience SAQ Training methods have made a huge impact on the performance of players in rugby and other sports. In Irish rugby we will be looking to SAQ Training methods for further and ongoing improvements in our player's movement abilities.

I would encourage all coaches who take the time to read this most informative book to also complete the practical SAQ education courses. You and your players will benefit enormously from the SAQ Programme.

Dr. Liam Hennessy
Director of Fitness, IRFU.

I have been fortunate in my playing career to have represented the British Lions Rugby Union Team and the Great Britain Rugby League Team. During the course of my playing the two codes I have come across a whole range of different coaching and conditioning methods, some of which I found stimulating and rewarding and some which I felt did not improve me as a player.

It therefore gives me pleasure to write this foreword as I have found the SAQ Programme both challenging and stimulating. More than that, it is relevant at all levels, for both codes and for player and

coach alike. I hope you enjoy the book and the opportunity it gives to make you a better player or coach.

Dai Young
Wales, British Lions, GB Rugby League

As a UK based, Premier Division rugby strength and conditioning coach I deal on a daily basis with international players as well as developing academy talent. I use SAQ Training as an important part of all my players' training programmes and they have all benefited from its use. I have also found SAQ Programmes to be very useful in the rehabilitation of injured players, allowing them to re-establish neuromuscular coordination and balance far more rapidly.

The great thing about SAQ Training is that it is fun, it can be adapted to any sport and you don't have to be a sports superstar to take advantage of it.

I thoroughly recommend SAQ Training to everyone, whatever your sport.

Mark Spivey
Strength and Conditioning Coach, Bath Rugby Club (formerly Bristol Rugby and England Women's Rugby)
National Decathlete

I really enjoy using the SAQ Programme as part of my training at both Bath Rugby and England Rugby. I feel that it has definitely contributed to my increased speed, balance and agility – and it's great fun at the same time.

Iain Balshaw
Bath Rugby, England Rugby, British Lions

Introduction

The Foundation of SAQ for Rugby

There is nothing more electrifying than a rugby player changing direction with precise, controlled side-steps, hitting an opponent with balanced force and then twisting out of a defensive tackle to explode through a gap in the defensive line and set up or score a try. The 6 foot 5 inch second row jumps and is then assisted into the air at a line out. He returns to the ground, turns, runs a support loop, side-steps to avoid bodies on the ground, receives a pass, gives a pass, and supports the play by using great agility to step over his team-mate to pick up the ball that has been placed on the ground.

Breathtakingly magnificent, rugby has got it all – speed, power, acceleration, agility, contact and lightning quick responses, all of which make it one of the most exciting and intensive games on earth. These acts of speed, agility and quickness are what makes the difference between winning and losing, success and failure. Often thought to be 'God given' gifts and therefore neglected on the training field, they are not only admired by coaches, trainers, players and supporters alike, but are deemed to be crucial aspects of the modern game of rugby.

The SAQ Programme for rugby is the first ever rugby-specific programme designed to develop these key skills. As well as being full of variety and great fun, the programme also has other significant benefits such as improving hand, eye and foot co-ordination, strength, explosive power and core control, which helps to prevent injury and aid rehabilitation.

The secret to SAQ success lies within the SAQ Continuum and the use of progressive and sequential learning techniques, breaking down complex sports science and delivering it in such a way that it is easy both to understand and to implement. The end result is the development of multi-directional explosive speed specifically for rugby. The SAQ Continuum is unique and can be adapted to meet the needs of both squad training and individual players within a squad who require position-specific development. The programme also provides an ideal opportunity for children as young as six, the most senior of professional players and the amateur who trains twice a week to learn and make improvements in all areas of their game.

What is SAQ Training?

In all sports – both team and individual – speed has been seen as a crucial commodity for many years. Commonly understood as how fast an object travels from point A to point B, speed is in fact a far more complex phenomenon. It is only recently that studies into speed, its various stages and their development have been carried out – identifying a number of areas, such as the start, the acceleration phase, the 'plaining out' phase and the finish, including effective deceleration. With such research, techniques such as stride frequency, stride length, 'jelly jaw' and holding your breath for the first 30 metres have been introduced. The many SAQ Training experts and practitioners involved in the development and delivery of SAQ Programmes have been committed to fill this void by developing all types of speed, particularly for team sports such as rugby. SAQ Programmes break speed down into three main areas of skill: speed, agility and quickness.

THE SAQ PROGRAMME'S FOUNDATION

SPEED

A crucial part of any player's game is the ability to cover the ground efficiently and economically over the first few metres, and then to open up stride length and increase stride frequency when working over 40–50 metres. Speed is defined as the maximum velocity a player can achieve and maintain; most humans can only maintain this maximum velocity for a short period of time and over a short distance. Speed can also be measured by the amount of time it takes a player to cover a particular distance.

Training to improve maximum speed requires a strong focus on correct running mechanics, stride length and frequency, the leg cycle and hip height/ position. Drills such as the 'dead leg run' (*see* page 37) and stride frequency drills that are used to help develop an economical running technique (*see* pp. 33–4) can all be easily integrated in a training session.

The best sprinters spend very little time in contact with the ground, and what contact they do make is extremely efficient and powerful. Focusing on the mechanics of running helps to control this power and use it efficiently and sparingly. Training when fresh is also crucial for an athlete or player to attain their maximum speed. Many athletes can only reproduce top speeds for a few weeks of the year, but the inclusion and practice of correct running mechanics on the training field will benefit players of the game greatly. How often do you see players accelerate onto a pass, control the ball then pass it on only to let their arms hang by their sides? Or the drills that have rugby players running with their hands out like Frankenstein ready to receive a pass? In both situations the player fails to re-assert good arm mechanics after a pass which can make the difference between getting to the next pass or missing out. Running with your arms out results in one-paced running and an inability to break through gaps in the opposition's defence. The correct arm mechanics and overall running techniques are therefore crucial in the development of explosive, balanced rugby players.

AGILITY

Agility is the ability to change direction without loss of balance, strength, speed or body control. There is a direct link between improved agility and the development of an individual's timing, rhythm and movement.

Agility should not be taken for granted and can actually be taught to individual players. Training ensures that a rugby player develops the best attacking and defensive skills possible with the greatest quickness, speed and control and the least amount of wasted energy and movement. Agility also has many other benefits for the individual, helping to prevent niggling injuries and teaching the muscles how to fire properly and control minute shifts in ankle, knee, hip, back, shoulder and neck joints for optimum body alignment. Imagine the type of agility a forward player requires to run at pace and to drop the body angle for a driving ruck, then to come upright, side-step and accelerate to the next position.

Another very important benefit of agility training is that it is long lasting. Unlike speed, stamina and weight training, it does not have to be maintained to retain the benefits. Consider the elderly person who can still ride a bicycle 40 years after having last ridden one. Agility training acts like an indelible mark, programming muscle memory.

THE ELEMENTS OF AGILITY

There are four elements to agility:

- balance
- co-ordination
- programmed agility
- random agility.

Within these there is speed, strength, timing and rhythm.

Balance is a foundation of athleticism. Here we teach the ability to stand, stop and walk by focusing on the centre of gravity – and it can be taught and retained relatively quickly. Examples include: standing on one leg; walking on a balance beam; standing on a balance beam; standing on an agility disc; walking backwards with your eyes closed; and jumping on a mini trampoline and then 'freezing'. It only requires a couple of minutes, two or three times a week to train balance – with the emphasis placed early in the morning and early in a training session when players are fresh and alert. This is when the nervous system and muscles are more receptive to patterns of movement used in balance.

Co-ordination is the goal of mastering simple skills under more difficult stresses. Co-ordination work is often slow and methodical, with an emphasis on correct biomechanics during athletically demanding movements. Training co-ordination can be completed by breaking a skill down into sections then gradually bringing them together. Co-ordination activities include footwork drills, tumbling, rolling and jumping. More difficult examples are walking on a balance beam while playing catch, running along a line while a partner lightly pulls and pushes in an attempt to move the player off the line, and jumping on and off an agility disc while holding a Jelly Ball.

The third element of agility training is called **'programmed' agility**. This is when a player has already experienced the skill or stress that is to be placed on him and is aware of the pattern and sequence of demands of that experience. In short, the player has already been programmed. Programmed agility drills can be conducted at high speeds but must be learnt at low, controlled speeds. Examples are zig-zag pick up and place runs (*see* page 72, 4-square ball (*see* page 68) and 'T'-runs (*see* page 69) all of which involve a change in direction along a known standardised pattern. The pattern of body height adjustment should also be practised here – drills that focus on straight and angled runs, where players have to drop their body height to simulate picking up the ball and driving rucks and mauls before returning to an upright position and re-asserting the arm and foot mechanics needed for acceleration. Once these types of drills are learnt and performed on a regular basis, times and performances will improve and advances in strength, explosion, flexibility and body control will be witnessed. This is true of players of any ability.

The final element – and the most difficult to master, prepare for and perform – is **random agility**. Here the player performs tasks with unknown patterns and unknown demands; the coach can incorporate visual and audible reactive skills so that the player has to make split-second decisions with movements based upon the various stimuli. The skill level is now becoming much closer to actual game-like situations. Random agility can be trained by games like tag, read and react (tennis ball drops and dodge), dodge ball and more specific training such as jumping and landing followed by an immediate, unknown movement demand from the coach.

Agility training is challenging, fun and exciting. There is the opportunity for tremendous variety, and training should not become boring or laborious. Agility is not just for those with elite sporting abilities; try navigating through a busy shopping mall!

QUICKNESS

As the ball is taken cleanly at the back of the line-out and from a standing position, the 17-stone blind-side flanker accelerates from the front of the line-out on an explosive loop to hit a perfectly timed pass and drive into the opposition territory. When a player accelerates like this, a great deal of force has to be generated and transferred through the foot to the ground. This action is similar to that when you roll a towel up (the 'leg'), hold one end in your hand and flick it out to achieve a 'cracking' noise from the other end (the 'foot'). The act of acceleration occurs in a fraction of a second and takes the body from a static position to motion. Muscles actually lengthen and then shorten instantaneously – that is an 'eccentric' followed by a 'concentric' contraction. This process is known as the stretch shortening cycle action (SCC). SAQ Training concentrates on improving the neuro-muscular system that impacts on this process, so that this initial movement – whether lateral, linear or vertical – is automatic, explosive and precise. The reaction time is the time it takes for the brain to receive and respond to a stimulus by sending a message to the muscle causing it to contract. This is what helps a centre explode through a gap, or the second row to make a dynamic line-out leap and a split-second catch before passing to the scrum half. With ongoing SAQ Training, the neuro-muscular system is reprogrammed and restrictive mental blocks and thresholds such as slow, unco-ordinated intitial acceleration and limited range of movement are removed or improved. For example, the player who automatically rolls back onto their heels before accelerating forward, wasting valuable time and energy. Consequently, messages from the brain have a clear path to the muscles so that the result is an instinctively quicker player.

Quickness training begins with 'innervation' (isolated fast contractions of an individual joint): for example, repeating the same explosive movement over a short period of time, such as fast feet and line drills. These quick, repetitive motions take the body through the gears, moving it in a co-ordinated manner to develop speed. Integrating quickness training throughout the year by using fast feet and reaction-type drills will result in the muscles having increased firing rates. This means that players are capable of faster, more controlled acceleration. The goal is to ensure that your players explode over the first 3–5 metres. Imagine that the firing between the nervous system and the muscles are the gears in a car; the timing, speed and smoothness of the gear-change cause the wheels – and thus the car – to accelerate away efficiently. Achieved with balance and co-ordination, the wheels do not spin and the car does not lose control.

MOVEMENT SKILLS

Many elements of balance and co-ordination involve the processing of sensory information from within the body. Proprioceptors are sensors that detect muscular tension, tension in tendons, relative body positions and pressure in the skin. In addition, the body has a range of other sensors that detect balance. The ability to express balance and co-ordination is highly dependent on the effectiveness of the body's internal sensors and proprioceptors, just like the suspension on a car. Through training, these sensors, and the neural communication system within the body become more effective. In addition, the brain becomes more able to interpret these messages and formulate the appropriate movement response. This physiological development underpins effective movement and future movement skill development.

SAQ Equipment

SAQ Equipment adds variety and stimuli to your training session. Drill variations are almost endless and once mastered, the results achieved can be quite astonishing. Players of all ages and abilities enjoy the challenges presented to them when training with SAQ Equipment, particularly when introduced in a rugby-specific manner.

When using SAQ Equipment, coaches, trainers and players must be aware of the safety issues involved – and of the reduced effectiveness and potentially dangerous consequence of using inappropriate or inferior equipment. Having said this, many of the drills can be performed using equipment that is readily available to most coaches – such as cones, garden canes and so on – always provided that safety and correct technique remain priorities. The following pages introduce a variety of SAQ Equipment recommended for use in many of the drills detailed later in this book.

FAST FOOT LADDERS

These are made of webbing with round, hard plastic rungs spaced approximately 45 cm apart. They come in sets of two pieces, each measuring 4.5 metres. The pieces can be joined together or used as two separate ladders; they can also be folded over to create different angles for players to perform drills on. Fast Foot Ladders are great for improving agility and for the development of explosive fast feet.

MICRO AND MACRO HURDLES

These come in two sizes: micro hurdles measuring 18 cm and macro hurdles measuring 30 cm in height. They are constructed of a hard plastic and have been specifically designed as a safe freestanding piece of equipment. It is recommended that the hurdles be used in sets of 6–8 to perform the mechanics drills detailed later. They are ideal for practising running mechanics and low-impact plyometrics. The micro hurdles are also great for lateral work.

SONIC CHUTE

This is constructed from webbing (the belt), nylon cord and a lightweight cloth 'chute', the size of which may vary from 1.5–1.8 m. The belts have a release mechanism that when pulled drops the chute so that the player can explode forwards. Sonic Chutes are great for developing sprint endurance.

VIPER BELT

This is a resistance belt specially made for high intensity training. It has three stainless steel anchor points where a flexi-cord can be attached. The flexi-cord is made from surgical tubing with a specific elongation. The Viper Belt has a safety belt and safety fasteners; it is double stitched and provides a good level of resistance. This piece of equipment is effective for developing explosive speed in all directions.

SIDE-STEPPERS

These are padded ankle straps that are connected together by an adjustable flexi-cord. They are effective in the development of lateral movements.

REACTION BALL

A rubber ball specifically shaped so that it bounces in unpredictable directions.

PUNCH/KICK RESISTOR

A padded cuff that can be worn around the ankle or the wrist with a flexi-cord attached to it. Designed to provide resistance particularly for punching and kicking development.

OVERSPEED TOW ROPE

The overspeed tow rope is made up of two belts and a 50-metre nylon cord pulley system. It can be used to provide resistance and is designed for the development of express overspeed and swerve running.

BREAK-AWAY BELT

These are webbing belts that are connected by Velcro-covered connecting strips. They are great for mirror drills and position-specific marking drills, breaking apart when one player gets away from the other.

STRIDE FREQUENCY CANES

Plastic, 1.2 m canes of different colours that are used to mark out stride patterns.

SPRINT SLED

This is a metal sledge with a centre area to accommodate different weights, and a running harness that is attached to the sledge by webbing straps of 8–10 metres in length.

JELLY BALLS

Round, soft rubber balls filled with a water-based 'jelly like' substance. They range in weight from 2–8 kg, and differ from the old-fashioned medicine balls because they can be bounced with great force onto hard surfaces.

HAND WEIGHTS

Foam-covered weights, each weighing between 0.7–1 kg. They are safe and easy to use both indoors and outdoors.

VISUAL ACUITY RING

A hard plastic ring of approx 75 cm diameter with four different-coloured balls attached to it, all equally distributed around the ring. The ring helps to develop visual acuity and tracking skills when thrown and caught between the players. This piece of equipment is effective for hand–eye co-ordination.

PERIPHERAL VISION STICK

This stick is simple but very effective for the training of peripheral vision. It is approximately 1.2 m long with a brightly coloured ball at one end. Once again, this is a great piece of equipment for eye–hand co-ordination.

BUNT BAT

A 1.2 metre stick with three coloured balls – one at each end and one in the middle. Working in pairs, one player (1) holds the bat with two hands while the other throws a small ball or bean bag for player 1 to 'bunt' or fend off. The Bunt Bat is effective for hand–eye co-ordination.

AGILITY DISC

An inflatable rubber disc 45 cm across, this piece of equipment is multi-purpose but particularly good for proprioreceptive and core development work (to strengthen the deep muscles of the trunk). Agility discs can be stood on, kneeled on, sat on and laid on for the performance of all types of exercises.

The SAQ Continuum

Team games such as rugby are characterised by explosive movements, acceleration and deceleration, agility, turning ability and speed of responses (Smythe 2000). The SAQ Continuum is the sequence and progression of components that make up a SAQ Training Session. The progressive elements include rugby-specific patterns of running and drills, including ball work. The continuum is also flexible, and once the pre-season foundation work has been completed – during the season when time and recovery are of the essence – short combination SAQ Training Sessions provide a constant top-up to the skills that have already been learned.

SAQ Training is like any other fitness training: if neglected, then players' explosive multi-directional power will diminish. The component parts of the SAQ Continuum and how they relate to rugby are as follows:

- **Dynamic Flex** – warm-up on the move

- **mechanics of movement** – the development of running form for rugby

- **innervation** – fast feet, agility and control for rugby

- **accumulation of potential** – the bringing together of the previous components in a SAQ training rugby circuit

- **explosion** – the development of explosive 3-step multi-directional acceleration for rugby

- **expression of potential** – short, competitive team games that prepare players for the next level of training

- **warm-down**

Throughout the continuum, position-specific drills and skills can be implemented.

CHAPTER 1 DYNAMIC FLEX

'WARM-UP ON THE MOVE'

It is common knowledge that before engaging in intense or strenuous exercise, the body should be prepared. The warm-up should achieve a change in a number of physiological responses, in order that the body can work safely and effectively:

- increase body temperature, specifically core (deep) muscle temperature

- increase heart rate and blood flow

- increase breathing rate

- increase the elasticity of muscular system

- activate the neuro-muscular system

- increase mental alertness.

The warm-up should take a player from a rested state to the physiological state required for participation in the session that is to follow. It should gradually increase in intensity as the session goes on; in addition, it should be fun and stimulating for the players, 'switching them on' mentally.

What is Dynamic Flex?

The standard training session for soccer begins by warming the players up before taking them through a series of stretches that focus on the main muscle groups in the body. However, 'static' stretches like this are not really relevant within a game of rugby. Players do not need to be able to do the splits like gymnasts and dancers, but they do need to be able to perform diving, jumping and agility movements. Dynamic Flex is what allows a rugby player to do this: flexibility in action, if you like, combined with power and strength.

Indeed, the most recent research has shown that static stretching before training or competition can actually be detrimental to performance. One study

found that the eccentric strength of the muscle – its strength when lengthening, for instance when a player brakes or lands from a jump – was reduced by 7–9% for up to an hour after static stretching. Similarly, it was discovered that there was a clear decrease in the peak power output of the muscle after stretching.

Dynamic stretching, by contrast, has been shown to increase muscle warmth, and therefore its elasticity. This is vital for performance and for muscle safety. One of the main arguments in favour of static stretching – that it helps to prevent injury – has also now been called into question, with recent research suggesting that it has almost no effect on injury prevention (Gleim & McHugh 1997). Similarly, an Australian army physiotherapist (Pope 1999) studied army recruits over the course of a year. He instructed half to warm up with static stretching, and half to warm up without any stretching at all. He found no differences in the incidence of injury between the two groups, suggesting that static stretching is of little benefit in the pre-exercise warm-up.

The warm-up

Using a standard 20 × 20 metre grid (*see* fig. 1.1 page 2). The following exercises represent a foundation set of Dynamic Flex warm-up drills. Also included in this chapter are variations and the introduction of the ball. It is important to remember that rugby players not only enjoy variety but also respond pro-actively on the field to variations in training. Once they have mastered the standard set, the introduction of new grids (*see* figs 1.2–1.6 pages 30–2) and combination work including the ball, tackle bags and shield will ensure maximum participation.

NB In a warm-up drill, start slow, rehearse the movements then increase the intensity.

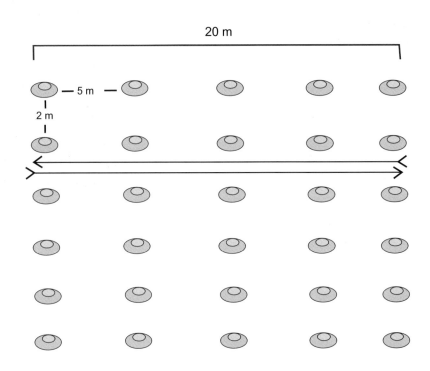

Figure 1.1 Standard grid

Key

Direction of running

DRILL   WALKING ON THE BALLS OF THE FEET

Aim
To stretch shins and improve ankle mobility. To improve balance and co-ordination. To increase body temperature.

Area/equipment
An indoor or outdoor grid 20 metres in length. The width of the grid is variable depending on the size of the squad (*see* fig. 1.1, Standard grid).

Description
Player to cover the length of the grid by walking on the balls of the feet. Return to the start by repeating the drill in a backward motion.

Key teaching points
- Do not walk on the ends of the toes
- Keep off the heels
- Maintain correct arm mechanics (*see* page 35)
- Maintain an upright posture

Sets and reps
2 × 20 metres, 1 forwards and 1 backwards.

Variations/progressions
Perform the drill laterally (in a sideways motion) but do not allow the feet to come together completely. Push off with the back foot, do not pull with the lead foot.

DRILL ANKLE FLICKS

Aim
To stretch calves and improve ankle mobility. To improve balance, co-ordination and rhythm of movement. To prepare for good foot-to-floor contact. To increase body temperature.

Area/equipment
An indoor or outdoor grid 20 metres in length. The width of the grid is variable depending on the size of the squad (*see* fig. 1.1).

Description
Player to cover the length of the grid in a 'skipping' type motion, where the balls of the feet plant then flick up towards the shin. The player should be seen to move in a bouncing manner. Return to the start by repeating the drill in a backward motion.

Key teaching points
- Work off the ball of the foot – not the toes
- Practise the first few steps on the spot before moving off
- Maintain correct arm mechanics (*see* page 35)
- Maintain an upright posture

Sets and reps
2 × 20 metres, 1 forwards and 1 backwards.

Variations/progressions
Perform the drill laterally.

DRILL   *KNEE TO CHEST*

Aim
To stretch the gluteals and to improve linear hip mobility. To increase body temperature.

Area/equipment
An indoor or outdoor grid 20 metres in length. The width of the grid is variable depending on the size of the squad (*see* fig. 1.1).

Description
The player stands tall and raises the knee of one leg up to the chest. To lightly increase the stretch, squeeze the knee in by placing the hands around the front of the knee and applying pressure. The foot is then returned to the ground and the drill is repeated on the other leg.

Key teaching points
- Work off the ball of the foot on the straight leg
- Apply pressure steadily
- Stay tall and look ahead

Sets and reps
2 x 20 metres, 1 forwards and 1 backwards.

Variations/progressions
On releasing the leg, use a knee-out skip (*see* page 13).

DRILL SMALL SKIPS

Aim
To increase lower leg flexibility and ankle mobility. To improve balance, co-ordination and rhythm, and develop positive foot-to-ground contact. To increase body temperature.

Area/equipment
An indoor or outdoor grid 20 metres in length. The width of the grid is variable depending on the size of the squad (*see* fig. 1.1).

Description
Player to cover the length of the grid in a low skipping motion. Return to the start by repeating the drill in a backward motion.

Key teaching points
- Knee to be raised to an angle of approximately 45–55°
- Work off the ball of the foot
- Maintain correct arm mechanics (*see* page 35)
- Maintain an upright posture
- Maintain a good rhythm

Sets and reps
2 x 20 metres, 1 forwards and 1 backwards.

Variations/progressions
Perform the drill laterally.

DRILL   WIDE SKIP

Aim
To improve hip and ankle mobility. To improve balance, co-ordination and rhythm. To increase body temperature.

Area/equipment
An indoor or outdoor grid 20 metres in length. The width of the grid is variable depending on the size of the squad (*see* fig. 1.1).

Drill description
Player to cover the length of the grid by skipping. The feet remain shoulder-width apart and knees face outwards at all times. Return to the start by repeating the drill in a backward motion.

Key teaching points
- Keep off the heels
- Maintain correct arm mechanics (*see* page 35)
- Maintain an upright posture
- Do not take the thigh above a 90° angle

Sets and reps
2 x 20 metres, 1 forwards and 1 backwards.

Variations/progressions
Perform the drill laterally.

DRILL **SINGLE KNEE DEAD-LEG LIFT**

Aim
To improve buttock flexibility and hip mobility. To isolate the correct 'running cycle' motion for each leg.

Area/equipment
An indoor or outdoor grid 20 metres in length. The width of the grid is variable depending on the size of the squad (*see* fig. 1.1).

Description
Player to cover the length of the grid by bringing the knee of one leg quickly up to a 90° position. The other leg should remain as straight as possible, with a very short lift away from the ground throughout the movement. The ratio should be 1:4, i.e. 1 lift to every 4 steps. Work one leg on the way down the grid and the other on the return.

Key teaching points
- Do not take the knee above the 90° angle
- Strike the floor with the ball of the foot
- Keep the foot facing forwards
- Maintain correct running mechanics (*see* pp. 33–34)

Sets and reps
2 x 20 metres, 1 forwards and 1 backwards.

Variations/progressions
Vary the lift ratio, e.g. 1:2.

DRILL   *HIGH KNEE-LIFT SKIP*

Aim

To improve buttock flexibility and hip mobility. To increase the range of motion (ROM) over a period of time. To develop rhythm and increase body temperature.

Area/equipment

An indoor or outdoor grid 20 metres in length. The width of the grid is variable depending on the size of the squad (*see* fig. 1.1).

Description

Player to cover the length of the grid in a high skipping motion. Return to the start by repeating the drill in a backward motion.

Key teaching points

- Thigh to be taken past 90°
- Work off the balls of the feet
- Maintain a strong core
- Maintain an upright posture
- Control the head by looking forwards at all times
- Maintain correct arm mechanics (*see* page 35)

Sets and reps

2 x 20 metres, 1 forwards and 1 backwards.

Variations/progressions

Perform the drill laterally.

DRILL KNEE-ACROSS SKIP

Aim
To increase outer hip flexibility and hip mobility, which will improve over a period of time. To develop balance and co-ordination. To increase body temperature.

Area/equipment
An indoor or outdoor grid 20 metres in length. The width of the grid is variable depending on the size of the squad (*see* fig. 1.1).

Description
Player to cover the length of the grid in a skipping motion where the knee comes across the body. Return to the start by repeating the drill in a backward motion.

Key teaching points
- Do not force an increased ROM
- Work off the balls of the feet
- Maintain a strong core
- Maintain an upright posture
- Control the head by looking forwards at all times
- Use the arms primarily for balance

Sets and reps
2 x 20 metres, 1 forwards and 1 backwards.

Variations/progressions
Perform the drill laterally.

DRILL | *LATERAL RUNNING*

Aim
To develop an economical knee drive. To stretch the quadriceps and prepare for an efficient lateral running technique. To increase body temperature.

Area/equipment
An indoor or outdoor grid 20 metres in length. The width of the grid is variable depending on the size of the squad (*see* fig. 1.1).

Description
Player to cover the length of the grid with the left or right shoulder leading, taking short lateral steps. Return with the opposite shoulder leading.

Key teaching points
- Keep the hips square
- Work off the balls of the feet
- Do not skip
- Do not let the feet cross over
- Maintain an upright posture
- Do not sink into the hips (*see* page 34) or bend over at the waist
- Do not overstride – use short, sharp steps
- Maintain correct arm mechanics (*see* page 35)

Sets and reps
2 x 20 metres, 1 left-shoulder lead and 1 right-shoulder lead.

Variations/progressions
Practise lateral angled zig-zag runs.

DRILL ICE SKATING

Aim
To increase hip and ankle mobility, lateral foot control, balance and co-ordination. To increase body temperature.

Area/equipment
An indoor or outdoor grid 20 metres in length. The width of the grid is variable depending on the size of the squad (*see* fig. 1.1).

Description
The player leans slightly forwards and swings the arms across the body while side-stepping from left to right like an 'ice skater'.

Key teaching points
- Keep the head up
- Do not sink into the hips (*see* page 34) or bend over at the waist
- Try to land on the balls of the feet

Sets and reps
2 x 20 metres, 1 left-shoulder lead and 1 right-shoulder lead.

Variations/progression
Alternate from short step to long step.

DRILL   *KNEE-OUT SKIP*

Aim

To stretch the inner thighs and improve hip mobility. To develop an angled knee drive, balance, co-ordination and rhythm. To increase body temperature.

Area/equipment

An indoor or outdoor grid 20 metres in length. The width of the grid is variable depending on the size of the squad (*see* fig. 1.1).

Description

Player to cover the length of the grid in a skipping motion. The knee moves laterally from the centre of the body to a position outside the body, before returning to the central position. Return to the start by repeating the drill in a backward motion.

Key teaching points

- Feet start facing forwards and move outwards as the knees are raised
- Work off the balls of the feet
- The knee is to be pushed out and back, not rolled out
- Maintain correct arm mechanics (*see* page 35)
- The movement should be smooth, not jerky

Sets and reps

2 x 20 metres, 1 forwards and 1 backwards.

Variations/progressions

Perform the drill laterally.

DRILL PRE-TURN

Aim
To prepare the hips for a turning action without committing the whole body. To increase body temperature. To improve body control.

Area/equipment
An indoor or outdoor grid 20 metres in length. The width of the grid is variable depending on the size of the squad (*see* fig. 1.1).

Description
Player to cover the length of the grid by performing a lateral movement. The heel of the back foot is moved to a position almost alongside the lead foot. Just before the feet come together, the lead foot is moved away sideways. Return to the start by repeating the drill, but lead with the opposite shoulder.

Key teaching points
- The back foot must not cross the lead foot
- Work off the balls of the feet
- Maintain correct arm mechanics (*see* page 35)
- Maintain an upright posture
- Do not sink into the hips or fold at the waist (*see* page 34)
- Do not use a high knee-lift; the angle should be below 90° and preferably no more than 45°

Sets and reps
2 x 20 metres, 1 left-shoulder lead and 1 right-shoulder lead.

DRILL   *RUSSIAN WALK*

Aim
To stretch the back of the thighs, improve hip mobility and stabilise the ankles. To develop balance and co-ordination. To increase body temperature.

Area/equipment
An indoor or outdoor grid 20 metres in length. The width of the grid is variable depending on the size of the squad (*see* fig. 1.1).

Description
Player to cover the length of the grid by performing a walking march with a high extended step. Imagine that the aim is to scrape the sole of your shoe down the front of a door.

Key teaching points
- Lift the knee before extending the leg
- Work off the balls of the feet
- Try to keep off the heels, particularly on the back foot
- Keep the hips square

Sets and reps
2 x 20 metres, both forwards.

Variations/progressions
Perform the drill backwards.

DRILL *WALKING LUNGE*

Aim
To stretch the front of the hips and thighs. To develop balance and co-ordination. To increase body temperature.

Area/equipment
An indoor or outdoor grid 20 metres in length. The width of the grid is variable depending on the size of the squad (*see* fig. 1.1).

Description
Player to cover the length of the grid by performing a walking lunge. The front leg should be bent with a 90° angle at the knee and the thigh in a horizontal position. The back leg should also be at a 90° angle but with the knee touching the ground and the thigh in a vertical position. Return to the start by repeating the drill in a backward motion.

Key teaching points
- Try to keep the hips square
- Maintain a strong core and keep upright
- Maintain good control
- Persevere with backward lunges – these are difficult to master

Sets and reps
2 x 20 metres, 1 forwards and 1 backwards.

Variations/progressions
- Perform the drill with hand weights
- Perform the drill while catching and passing a ball in the down position

DRILL · SIDE LUNGE

Aim
To stretch inner thighs and gluteals (buttocks). To develop balance and co-ordination. To increase body temperature.

Area/equipment
An indoor or outdoor grid 20 metres in length. The width of the grid is variable depending on the size of the squad (*see* fig. 1.1).

Description
Player to cover the length of the grid by performing lateral lunges. Take a wide lateral step and simultaneously lower the gluteals towards the ground. Return to the start with the opposite shoulder leading.

Key teaching points
- Do not bend at the waist or lean forwards
- Try to keep off the heels
- Maintain a strong core and a straight spine
- Use the arms primarily for balance

Sets and reps
2 x 20 metres, 1 left-shoulder leading and 1 right-shoulder leading.

Variations/progressions
Work in pairs facing each other and chest-passing the ball.

DRILL   *HURDLE WALK*

Aim
To stretch inner and outer thighs and increase ROM. To develop balance and co-ordination. To increase body temperature.

Area/equipment
An indoor or outdoor grid 20 metres in length. The width of the grid is variable depending on the size of the squad.

Description
Player to cover the length of the grid by walking in a straight line and alternating the lifting leg as if going over a high hurdle. Return to the start by repeating the drill in a backwards motion.

Key teaching points
- Try to keep the body square as the hips rotate
- Work off the balls of the feet
- Maintain an upright posture
- Do not sink into the hips or bend over at the waist (*see* page 34)
- Imagine that you are actually stepping over a barrier

Sets and reps
2 x 20 metres, 1 forwards and 1 backwards.

DRILL 'TWIST AGAIN'

Aim
To improve rotational hip mobility and speed. To develop balance, foot control and co-ordination. To increase body temperature.

Area/equipment
An indoor or outdoor grid 20 metres in length. The width of the grid is variable depending on the size of the squad (*see* fig. 1.1).

Description
The player stands tall with his feet together, and then jumps forwards – moving the feet to the left and then across the body to the right. The arms should be fired across the body for balance and speed.

Key teaching points
- Try to develop a rhythm
- Work off the balls of the feet
- Maintain an upright posture and look ahead
- Do not sink into the hips or bend over at the waist (*see* page 34)

Sets and reps
2 x 20 metres, 1 forwards and 1 backwards.

Variations/progressions
Perform the drill sideways, changing from left to right shoulders.

DRILL WALKING HAMSTRING

Aim
To stretch the backs of the thighs. To increase body temperature.

Area/equipment
An indoor or outdoor grid 20 metres in length. The width of the grid is variable depending on the size of the squad (*see* fig. 1.1).

Description
Player to cover the length of the grid by extending the lead-leg heel first on to the ground and then rolling on to the ball of the foot. Walk forwards and repeat on the opposite leg. Continue in this manner alternating the lead leg.

Key teaching points
- Keep the spine in a straight line
- Do not arch the back but lean into the stretch from the hips
- Control the head by looking forwards at all times
- Work at a steady pace, do not rush

Sets and reps
2 x 20 metres, 1 forwards and 1 backwards.

DRILL   *HAMSTRING BUTTOCK FLICKS*

Aim
To stretch the front and back of the quadriceps. To improve hip mobility. To increase body temperature.

Area/equipment
An indoor or outdoor grid 20 metres in length. The width of the grid is variable depending on the size of the squad (*see* fig. 1.1).

Description
Player to cover the length of the grid by moving forwards alternating leg flicks where the heel moves up towards the buttocks. Return to the start by repeating the drill in a backwards motion.

Key teaching points
- Start slowly and build up the tempo
- Work off the balls of the feet
- Maintain an upright posture
- Do not sink into the hips (*see* page 34)
- Try to develop a rhythm

Sets and reps
2 x 20 metres, 1 forwards and 1 backwards.

Variations/progressions
- Perform the drill laterally
- Perform the drill as above, but flick the heel to the *outside* of the buttocks

DRILL   CARIOCA

Aim

To improve hip mobility and speed, which will increase the firing of nerve impulses over a period of time. To develop balance and co-ordination while moving and twisting. To increase body temperature.

Area/equipment

An indoor or outdoor grid 20 metres in length. The width of the grid is variable depending on the size of the squad (*see* fig. 1.1).

Description

Player to cover the length of the grid by moving laterally. The rear foot crosses in front of the body and then moves around to the back of the body. Simultaneously, the lead foot will do the opposite. The arms also move across the front and back of the body.

Key teaching points

- Start slowly and build up the tempo
- Work off the balls of the feet
- Keep the shoulders square
- Do not force the ROM
- Use the arms primarily for balance

Sets and reps

2 x 20 metres, 1 left-leg leading and 1 right-leg leading.

Variations/progressions

Perform the drill with a partner (mirror drills) – i.e. one initiates or leads the movement while the other attempts to follow.

DRILL   *WALL DRILLS – LEG ACROSS BODY*

Aim
To increase the ROM in the hip region. To increase body temperature.

Area/equipment
A wall or fence to lean against.

Description
The player faces and leans against the wall or fence at an angle of approximately 20–30°. Swing the leg across the body from one side to the other. Repeat on the other leg.

Key teaching points
- Do not force an increased ROM
- Work off the ball of the support foot
- Lean with both hands against the wall or fence
- Keep the hips square
- Gradually speed up the movement

Sets and reps
7–10 on each leg. Players to work one leg and then alternate.

Variations/progression
Lean against a partner as shown – but being careful how the leg is swung!.

DRILL WALL DRILLS – LINEAR LEG SWING

Aim
To increase the ROM in the hip region. To increase body temperature.

Area/equipment
A wall or fence to lean against.

Description
The player faces and leans against the wall or fence at an angle of approximately 20–30°. Take the leg back and swing it forwards in a linear motion along the same plane. Repeat on the other leg.

Key teaching points
- Do not force an increased ROM
- Work off the ball of the support foot
- Lean with both hands against the wall or fence
- Do not look down
- Gradually speed up the movement

Sets and reps
7–10 on each leg. Players to work one leg and then alternate.

Variations/progressions
Lean against a partner.

DRILL WALL DRILLS – KNEE ACROSS BODY

Aim
To increase the ROM in the hip region. To increase body temperature.

Area/equipment
A wall or fence to lean against.

Description
The player faces and leans against the wall or fence at an angle of approximately 20–30°. From a standing position, drive one knee upwards and across the body. Repeat on the other leg.

Key teaching points
- Do not force an increased ROM
- Work off the ball of the support foot
- Lean with both hands against the wall or fence
- Keep the hips square
- Gradually speed up the movement
- Imagine you are trying to get your knee up and across the body to the opposite hip region

Sets and reps
7–10 on each leg. Players to work one leg then alternate.

Variations/progressions
Lean against a partner as shown – being careful how you raise your knee!.

DRILL | WALL DRILLS – HIP THRUSTS

Aim

To increase the ROM in the hip region. To stretch the thigh, calf and lower back with a resultant increase in body temperature.

Area/equipment

A wall or fence to lean against.

Description

The player faces and leans against the wall or fence at an angle of approximately 20–30°. From a standing position and keeping the spine straight, bend the knees to approximately 45° then thrust upwards, bringing the hips up towards the wall and finishing on the balls of the feet.

Key teaching points

- Keep the spine in a straight line
- Do not sink into the hips (*see* page 34)
- Bend at the knees and not at the waist
- Try to develop a rhythm
- Do not look down

Sets and reps

7–10 thrusts.

Variations/progressions

Lean against a partner.

DRILL PAIR DRILLS – LATERAL RUNS

Aim
To develop running skills in a more game-specific situation. To simulate balance and co-ordination. To practise re-assertion of the correct mechanics from an unbalanced position. To increase body temperature.

Area/equipment
An indoor or outdoor grid 20 metres in length. The width of the grid is variable depending on the size of the squad.

Description
The players face each other approximately 0.5–1 metre apart and cover the length of the grid sideways taking short lateral steps. Occasionally one can push the other.

Key teaching points
- Refer to lateral running drills (*see* page 11)
- When off balance or after being pushed, the focus should be on a re-assertion of the correct arm and foot mechanics

Sets and reps
2 x 20 metres, 1 left-leg leading and 1 right-leg leading.

Variations/progressions
Introduce the ball and pass hand-to-hand.

DRILL PAIR DRILLS – JOCKEYING

Aim
To simulate defensive and attacking close-quarter movement patterns.
To increase body temperature.

Area/equipment
An indoor or outdoor grid 20 metres in length. The width of the grid
is variable depending on the size of the squad.

Description
Players to stand facing each other and cover the grid working both
forwards and backwards. The player moving forwards (attacker)
shows his left shoulder and then his right shoulder alternately in a
rhythmic motion. The player moving backwards (defender) mirrors
the attacking player's movements.

Key teaching points
- Take short steps
- Do not cross the feet
- Maintain a strong core and an upright posture
- Do not sink into the hips (*see* page 34)
- Keep your eyes on the opponent at all times

Sets and reps
2 x 20 metres, 1 left-leg leading and 1 right-leg leading.

Variations/progressions
Introduce the ball to the attacking player who presses with the ball in
his hands, transferring it from left to right to keep the defender on his
toes.

DRILL   *SELECTION OF SPRINTS*

Aim
To increase the intensity of the warm-up and prepare players for maximum exertion. To speed up the firing rate of neuro-muscular messages and increase body temperature.

Area/equipment
An indoor or outdoor grid 20 metres in length. The width of the grid is variable depending on the size of the squad. Only sprint one way; perform a jog-back recovery on the outside of the grid.

Description
Players to start from different angles – e.g. side-on, backwards, etc. – and to accelerate into a forward running motion down the grid.

Key teaching points
- Maintain good running mechanics (*see* pp. 33–34)
- Ensure that players alternate the lead foot

Sets and reps
1 set of 5 sprints, varying the start position.

Variations/progressions
- Include swerving sprints
- Include turns in the sprints

DRILL GRID VARIATIONS

Grid variations can be used to challenge and stimulate the players with a variety of movement patterns. These variations help to prevent players from becoming over-familiar with drills, which often leads to complacency. The following grid variations are examples only – feel free to use your imagination and design your own.

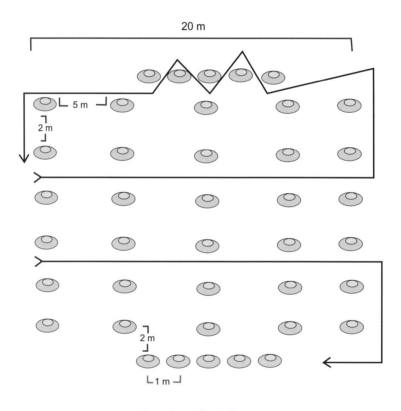

Figure 1.2 Grid variations

Key

Direction of running ⟶

GRID VARIATIONS

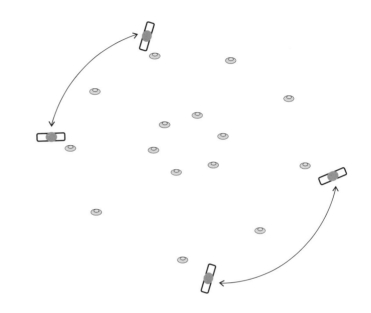

Figure 1.3 Dynamic Flex circle grid

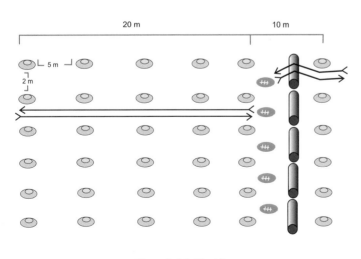

Figure 1.4 Split grid

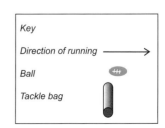

COMBINATION WARM-UP GRIDS

Many coaches are pushed for time during a busy season, the combination warm-up provides an effective and efficient method in preparing the players for the training session ahead. The combination warm-up not only covers the basics, it incorporates Dynamic Flex, fast feet, running mechanics and rugby specific movements – thus perfectly preparing the athlete for the more technical phase of the training session.

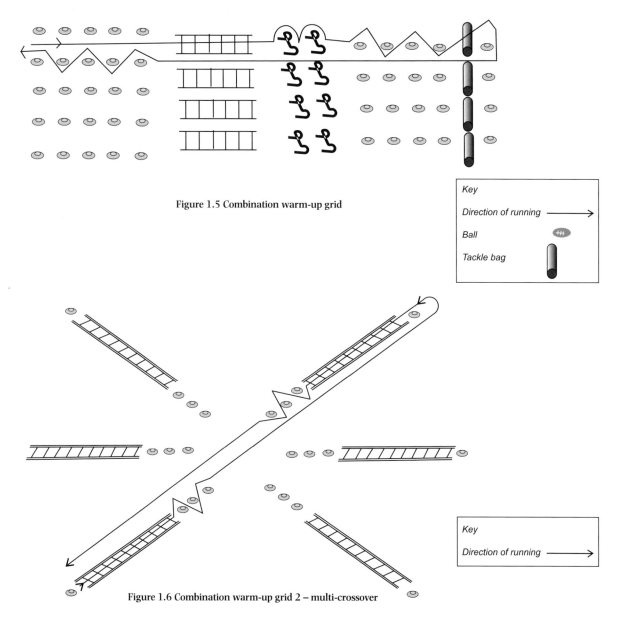

Figure 1.5 Combination warm-up grid

Key

Direction of running ⟶

Ball

Tackle bag

Figure 1.6 Combination warm-up grid 2 – multi-crossover

Key

Direction of running ⟶

CHAPTER 2 RUGBY RUNNING FORM

MECHANICS OF MOVEMENT

Rugby players are unique with regard to running form due to the fact that they have to handle the ball and use different angles for tackling, rucking and mauling during a game. Rugby requires a sound basic technique, as well as the ability to change from correct running mechanics to hold off a player, use the arms for balance when swerving at speed and re-assert good mechanics to re-accelerate. There is no need to focus on techniques for the 100 m sprint: rugby players very rarely have the space to plain out after 30 m or relax and think about 'jelly jaw' techniques – although practising the change of body height and using a strong arm drive is very important.

Arm mechanics

- elbows held at 90°
- hands relaxed
- the inside of the wrist should brush against your pockets
- the hand should move from the buttock cheek to the chest
- re-assert the arm drive as soon as possible after passing the ball or coming up from a lowered body position

Lift mechanics

Rugby is a multi-sprint, stop-and-start contact sport, so the first phase of acceleration and re-acceleration is crucial. Over the years, many players – and particularly the big forwards – have been coached to run with a high knee action. This was for two reasons: speed of acceleration, and making them a hard target to tackle. In actual fact, coaching players to get their knees up high, especially in the first few metres of the acceleration phase, only makes them slower and has the negative effect of minimising force development, so that insufficient power is produced to propel the body forwards in an explosive action. During the first few metres of acceleration short, sharp steps are required. These steps generate a high degree of force that takes the body from a stationary position into the first controlled explosive steps.

The acceleration phase is the process of taking the body from a stationary position to its maximum speed. The first 5 m are crucial because this is when a great deal of energy, force and power are used to propel the body forwards. During this initial phase emphasis should be placed on a short stride length and a high stride frequency. As the player accelerates, stride length will increase and the frequencey will decrease resulting in a greater distance being covered with each stride until maximum speed is reached. Correct stride length and stride frequency are vital for effective and efficient running. It is important that players be encouraged to shorten their stride length and increase the frequency when coming into the tackle zone, since this maximises foot-to-ground contact. This in turn allows the player to remain in control of their power and direction, enabling them to turn, twist, side-step, hit, bounce off and re-accelerate through the gaps. If a player maintains a long stride and a relatively low stride frequency, there will be less foot-to-ground contact; therefore, when the player is tackled either head-on or sideways-on, the likelihood of them being knocked backwards or to the ground is far greater. Look and listen for the following:

Initial acceleration strides

- 45° knee-lift
- foot contact to the floor with the ball of the foot
- front of the foot in a linear position
- knees come up in a vertical line
- foot-to-floor contact makes a tapping noise, not a thud or a slap
- if the foot or the knee splays in or out, this means that power will not be transferred correctly
- keep off the heels
- on the lift, the foot will transfer from pointing slightly down to pointing slightly up

Posture

Posture is also an important part of acceleration and sprinting. The spine should be kept straight as much as possible at all times. This means that a player who has tackled, side-stepped or jumped for the ball and now needs to run into space, needs to transfer to the correct running form as quickly as possible. Running with a straight spine does not mean running bolt upright; you can keep your spine straight using a slight lean forwards. What is to be avoided is players sinking into their hips, which looks like running 'folded up at the middle', because this prevents the effective transfer of power.

Body position

Rugby demands that the body position be lowered, particularly in contact situations, rucks and mauls, and when placing or picking the ball up. It is impossible for the human body to accelerate when in a lowered or bent position – so insisting that your players run and stay low, particularly the forwards, will in fact make them slower and less powerful. Instead, after lowering the body to perform a task,

the player must practise getting as tall as possible as quickly as possible. Looking up and firing the arms helps with this process.

Mechanics for deceleration

The ability of rugby players to stop quickly, change direction and accelerate is a key area in building successful teams. You can practise this: do not leave it to chance, include it in your sessions.

- *Posture* – lean back, this alters the angle of the spine and hips which control foot placement. Foot contact with the ground will now transfer to the heel, which acts like a brake.
- *Fire arms* – by firing the arms quickly, the energy produced will increase the frequency of heel contact with the ground. Think of it like pressing harder on the brakes in a car.

The running techniques described in this chapter cover basic mechanics for rugby-specific techniques, where running, pushing, jumping and turning are all important parts of the game. These are developed through the use of hurdles, stride frequency canes and practice of the correct running form.

Mechanics for jumping

As with running, arm drive is crucial for an efficient jumping technique. Both arms should move together through an arc from the hips to the ears in an explosive, upward, driving motion. This technique raises the body's centre of gravity – transferring a downward force through the hips and legs into an upward force that enables maximal upward thrust. The art is to maintain an upright position, use only a slight bend at the knees and simultaneously power off the balls of the feet. It is important to remember not to sink too deep in to the hips on landing as this will prevent a quick repeat jump or acceleration away from the landing.

DRILL ARM MECHANICS – MIRROR/PARTNER

Aim
To perfect the correct arm technique for running in rugby.

Area/equipment
A large mirror.

For partner drill – work with a partner.

Description
The player stands in front of the mirror with his arms 'ready' for sprinting and performs short bursts of arm drives. Use the mirror as a feedback tool to perfect the technique.

For partner drill – The player stands with their partner behind them. The partner holds the palms of his hand in line with the player's elbows, fingers pointing upwards. The player fires the arms as if sprinting so that the elbows 'smack' into the partner's palms.

Key teaching points
- The arms should not move across the body
- Keep the elbows at 90°
- The hands and shoulders should be relaxed
- The inside of the wrists should brush against the pockets
- ROM – the hands should move from buttock cheek to chest or head
- Ensure that the player performs a full ROM

Sets and reps
3 sets of 16 reps with 1 minute recovery between each set.

Variations/progressions
- Use light hand weights for the first 2 sets, controlling the movement carefully on the upswing; perform the last set without weights
- Introduce the ball to one side and practise arm mechanics while in possession of the ball

DRILL ARM MECHANICS – BUTTOCK BOUNCES

Aim
To develop explosive arm drive.

Area/equipment
A suitable ground surface.

Description
The player sits on the floor with his legs straight out in front of him. The arms are fired rapidly in short bursts. The power generated should be great enough to raise the buttocks off the floor in a bouncing manner.

Key teaching points
- The arms should not move across the body
- The elbows should be at 90°
- Keep the hands and shoulders relaxed
- The inside of the wrists should brush against the pockets
- ROM – the hands should move from buttock cheek to chest or head
- Encourage power in the movement

Sets and reps
3 sets of 6 reps. Each rep is 6–8 explosive arm drives with 1 minute recovery between each set.

Variations/progressions
Use light hand weights for the first 2 sets, controlling the movement carefully on the upswings; perform the last set without hand weights.

DRILL   *RUNNING FORM – DEAD-LEG RUN*

Aim
To develop a quick knee-lift and the positive foot placement required for effective sprinting.

Area/equipment
Indoor or outdoor area. Using hurdles, cones or sticks, place approximately 8 obstacles in a straight line at 0.5-metre intervals. Place a cone 1 metre from each end of the line to mark a start and finish.

Description
The player must keep the outside leg straight in a 'locked' position. The inside leg moves over the obstacles in a 'cycle'-like motion while the outside leg swings along just above the ground (*see* fig. 2.1).

Key teaching points
- Bring the knee of the inside leg up to just below 90°
- Point the toe upwards
- Bring the inside leg back down quickly between the hurdles
- Increase the speed when the technique has been mastered
- Maintain correct arm mechanics
- Maintain an upright posture
- Keep the hips square and stand tall

Sets and reps
1 set of 6 reps, 3 leading off the left leg and 3 leading off the right leg.

Variations/progressions
Use light hand weights – accelerate off the end of the last obstacle and drop the hand weights during this acceleration phase.

Key	
Left foot	
Right foot	
Direction of movement	⟶

Figure 2.1 Single dead-leg run

DRILL   RUNNING FORM – PRE-TURN

Aim
To educate and prepare the hips, legs and feet for effective and quick turning without fully committing the whole body.

Area/equipment
Indoor or outdoor area. Using hurdles, cones or sticks, place approximately 8 obstacles in a straight line at 0.5-metre intervals. Place a cone 1 metre from each end of the line to mark a start and finish.

Description
The player moves sideways along the line of obstacles just behind them (i.e. not travelling over them) (*see* fig. 2.2). The back leg (following leg) is brought over the hurdle to a position slightly in front of the body, so that the heel is in line with the toe of the leading foot. As the back foot is planted, the leading foot moves away. Repeat the drill leading with the opposite leg.

Key teaching points
- Stand tall, do not sink into the hips
- Do not allow the feet to cross over
- Keep the feet shoulder-width apart as much as possible
- The knee-lift should be no greater than 45°
- Maintain correct arm mechanics
- Maintain an upright posture
- Keep the hips and shoulders square
- Work both the left and right sides

Sets and reps
1 set of 6 reps, 3 leading with the left shoulder and 3 leading with the right shoulder.

Variations/progressions
Use light hand weights – at the end of the obstacles, turn and accelerate 5 metres. Drop the weights halfway through the acceleration phase.

Key	
Left foot	
Right foot	
Direction of movement	→

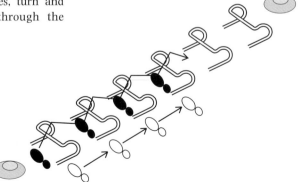

Figure 2.2 Pre-turn

DRILL   *RUNNING FORM – LEADING LEG RUN*

Aim
To develop quick, efficient steps and running technique.

Area/equipment
Indoor or outdoor area. Using hurdles, cones or sticks, place approximately 8 obstacles in a straight line at 0.5-metre intervals. Place a cone 1 metre from each end of the line to mark a start and finish.

Description
The player runs down the line of obstacles, crossing over each one with the same lead leg (*see* fig. 2.3). The player should aim to just clear the obstacles. Repeat the drill using the opposite leg as the lead.

Key teaching points
- Knee-drive should be no more than 45°
- Use short, sharp steps
- Maintain strong arm mechanics
- Maintain an upright posture: stand tall and do not sink into the hips

Sets and reps
1 set of 6 reps, 3 leading with the left leg and 3 leading with the right leg.

Variations/progressions
This is great for changing direction after running in a straight line. Place 3 cones at the end of the obstacles, at different angles and approximately 2–3 metres away. On leaving the last obstacle, the player sprints out to the cone nominated by the coach.

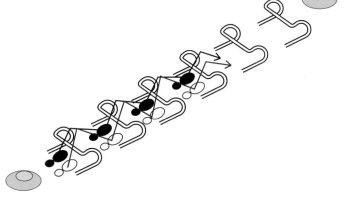

Key	
Left foot	
Right foot	
Leading foot	
Following foot	

Figure 2.3 Left- and right-leg lead

DRILL   *RUNNING FORM – LATERAL STEPPING*

Aim
To develop efficient and economical lateral steps.

Area/equipment
Indoor or outdoor area. Using hurdles, cones or sticks, place approximately 8 obstacles in a straight line at 0.5-metre intervals. Place a cone 1 metre from each end of the line to mark a start and finish.

Description
The player steps over each obstacle while moving sideways (*see* fig. 2.4).

Key teaching points
- Bring the knee up to just below 45°
- Do not skip sideways – step!
- Push off from the back foot
- Do not pull with the lead foot
- Maintain correct arm mechanics
- Maintain an upright posture
- Keep the hips square
- Do not sink into the hips

Sets and reps
1 set of 6 reps, 3 leading with the left shoulder and 3 leading with the right shoulder.

Variations/progressions
Use light hand weights – accelerate off the end of the last obstacle and drop the hand weights during this acceleration phase.

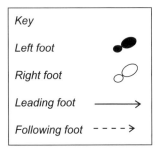

Key	
Left foot	●●
Right foot	○○
Leading foot	⟶
Following foot	⇢

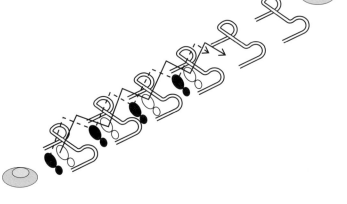

Figure 2.4 Lateral stepping

DRILL   RUNNING FORM – 1-2-3 LIFT

Aim
To develop an efficient leg cycle, rhythm, power and foot placement.

Area/equipment
Indoor or outdoor area – 30–40 metres long.

Description
The player moves in a straight line and after every third step the leg is brought up in an explosive action to 90°. Continue the drill along the length prescribed working the same leg, and then repeat the drill leading with the opposite leg.

Key teaching points
- Keep the hips square
- Work off the balls of the feet
- Try to develop and maintain a rhythm
- Keep eyes and head up and look ahead
- Maintain correct arm mechanics
- Maintain an upright posture
- Keep the hips square

Sets and reps
1 set of 6 reps, 3 leading with the left leg and 3 leading with the right leg.

Variations/progressions
- Alternate the lead leg during a repetition
- Vary the lift sequence, e.g. 1-2-3-4-lift, etc.

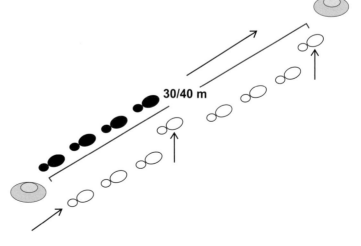

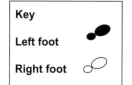

Key	
Left foot	
Right foot	

30/40 m

Figure 2.5 1-2-3 lift

DRILL *JUMPING – TWO-FOOTED SINGLES*

Aim
To develop jumping technique, power, speed and control.

Area/equipment
Indoor or outdoor area – ensure that the surface is clear of any obstacles. Use 18 cm or 30 cm hurdles.

Description
The player jumps over a single hurdle and on landing walks back to the start point to repeat the drill.

Key teaching points
- Maintain good arm mechanics
- Do not sink into the hips at the take-off and landing phases
- Land on the balls of the feet
- Do not fall back onto the heels

Sets and reps
2 sets of 8 reps with 1 minute recovery between each set.

Variations/progressions
- Single jumps over the hurdle and back – *see* fig. 2.6a
- Single jump over the hurdle with a 180° twist (**NB**: practise twisting to both sides – *see* fig. 2.6b)
- Lateral single jumps – use both sides to jump off (*see* fig. 2.6c)

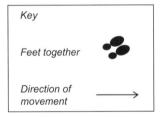

Key

Feet together

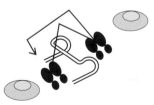

Direction of movement

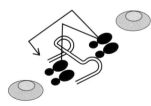

Figure 2.6(a) Two-footed single jump

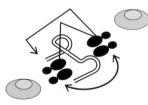

Figure 2.6(b) Two-footed single jump with 180° twist

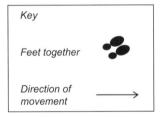

Figure 2.6(c) Two-footed lateral single jump

DRILL *JUMPING – MULTIPLE JUMPS*

Aim
To develop maximum control while taking off and landing. To develop controlled directional power.

Area/equipment
Indoor or outdoor area – 6–8 hurdles either 18 cm or 30 cm high. Place these at 0.5-metre intervals in a straight line.

Description
The player jumps over each hurdle in quick succession until all hurdles have been cleared. Walk back to the start and repeat the drill.

Key teaching points
- Use quick, rhythmic arm mechanics
- Do not sink into the hips at the take-off and landing phases
- Land and take off from the balls of the feet
- Stand tall and look straight ahead
- Maintain control
- Gradually build up the speed

Sets and reps
2 sets of 6 reps with 1 minute recovery between each set.

Variations/progressions
- Lateral jumps (*see* fig. 2.7b)
- Jumps with a 180° twist (*see* fig. 2.7c). **NB**: practise twisting to both sides.
- Hop over the hurdles, balance and then repeat (*see* fig. 2.7d)
- Use light hand weights – for the last rep of each of these sets, perform the drill without the weights as a contrast
- Introduce the ball – pass – catch and return

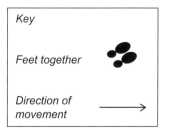

Key

Feet together

Direction of movement

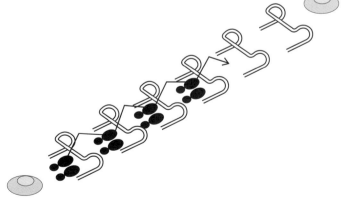

Figure 2.7(a) Multiple jumps

JUMPING – MULTIPLE JUMPS

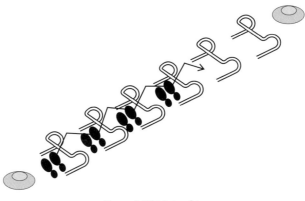

Figure 2.7(b) Lateral jumps

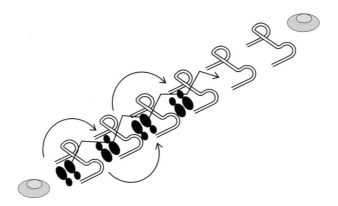

Figure 2.7(c) Jump with 180° twist

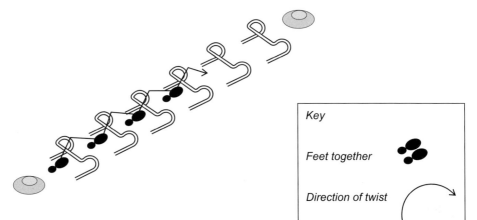

Figure 2.7(d) Jump with multiple hop

Key

Feet together

Direction of twist

DRILL
RUNNING FORM –
STRIDE FREQUENCY AND STRIDE LENGTH

Aim
To practise the transfer from the acceleration phase to an increase in stride frequency and length required when running. To develop an efficient leg cycle, rhythm, power and foot placement.

Area/equipment
Indoor or outdoor area – 40–60 metres long. 12 coloured sticks or canes 1.2 metres in length are placed out on the ground at intervals of 1.5–1.8 m (the intervals will be determined by the size and age of the group you are working with).

Description
Starting 20 metres away from the first stick or cane, the player accelerates towards the obstacle and on reaching it steps just over it. The player then continues with a measured stride frequency and length as dictated by the obstacles. On leaving the last stick or cane, the player gradually decelerates. Return to the start and repeat the drill.

Key teaching points
- Do not overstride
- Work off the balls of the feet
- Try to develop and maintain a rhythm
- Keep eyes/head up as if looking over a fence
- Maintain correct mechanics
- Maintain an upright posture
- Stay focused

Sets and reps
1 set of 4 reps.

Variations/progressions
- Set up the stride frequency sticks as shown in fig. 2.8. The sticks now control the acceleration and deceleration phases
- Add a change of direction during the deceleration phase.
- Add a ball during the deceleration and direction-change phase.

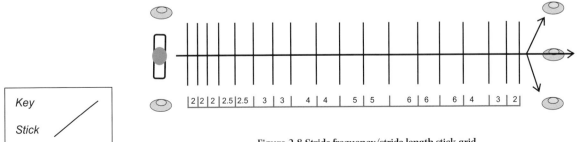

Key
Stick

Figure 2.8 Stride frequency/stride length stick grid

DRILL | RUNNING FORM – WITH A BALL

Aim

To maintain good mechanics when faced with rugby-specific stresses with the inclusion of a ball. To improve decision-making ability.

Area/equipment

Indoor or outdoor area – place 8 hurdles in a straight line at 0.5-metre intervals. Place a cone at each end approximately 2 metres from the first and last cones respectively.

Description

The coach stands at the end cone with the rugby ball. The player performs any of the above mechanics drills through the hurdles, and on clearing the final hurdle accelerates on to the ball that has been passed at various angles by the coach (*see* fig. 2.9a).

Key teaching points

- Maintain correct mechanics
- Stay focused by looking ahead
- Fire the arms explosively when accelerating to the ball

Sets and reps

3 sets of 6 reps. (**NB**: The sets should be made up of various mechanics drills.)

Variations/progressions

- On clearing the final hurdle, the player receives a pass from a player or coach on one side who transfers the ball across his body and passes to another player/coach who is positioned on the other side (*see* fig. 2.9b)
- The player performs lateral mechanics with his back to the shields and balls that are placed 2 metres away. On the coach's call the player turns and accelerates to the left or right to the nominated ball, picks it up, contacts the shield, performs a 360° twist and accelerates away (*see* fig. 2.9c)
- On clearing the final hurdle, the player receives a pass and accelerates on to hit a contact shield, then twists 360° before sprinting away (*see* fig. 2.9d)

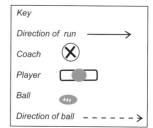

Key	
Direction of run	→
Coach	Ⓧ
Player	▭
Ball	⬭
Direction of ball	- - - →

Figure 2.9(a) Running mechanics with ball

RUNNING FORM – WITH A BALL contd.

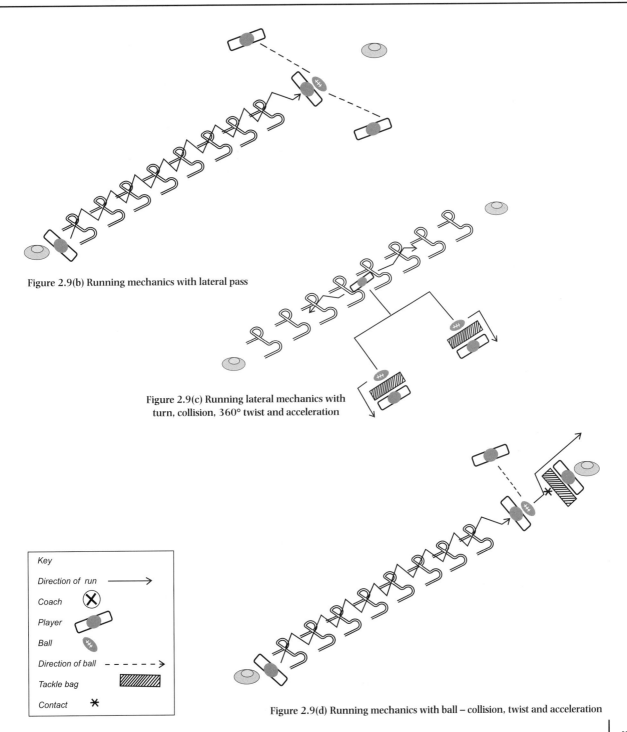

Figure 2.9(b) Running mechanics with lateral pass

Figure 2.9(c) Running lateral mechanics with
turn, collision, 360° twist and acceleration

Key

Direction of run	⟶
Coach	Ⓧ
Player	
Ball	
Direction of ball	- - - ->
Tackle bag	
Contact	✱

Figure 2.9(d) Running mechanics with ball – collision, twist and acceleration

DRILL   RUNNING FORM – HURDLE MIRROR DRILLS

Aim
To improve the performance of mechanics under pressure. To improve random agility.

Area/equipment
Indoor or outdoor area – mark out a grid with 2 lines of 8 hurdles with 2 hurdle lengths between each hurdle and about 2 metres between each line of hurdles (*see* fig. 2.10a).

Description
Players face each other while performing mechanics drills up and down the lines of hurdles. One player initiates the movements while the partner attempts to mirror them. Players can perform both lateral and linear mirror drills.

Key teaching points
- Stay focused on your partner
- The player mirroring should try to anticipate the lead player's movements
- Maintain correct arm mechanics

Sets and reps
Each player performs 3 sets of 30 second work periods. Ensure 30 second recovery between each work period

Variations/progressions
- First to the ball drills – performed as above except a ball is placed between the two lines of hurdles. The proactive partner commences the drill as normal then accelerates to the ball and either dives on it to secure the ball or scoops it up. The reactive player attempts to beat the proactive player to the ball (*see* fig. 2.10b)
- Lateral drills performed as above – players work in pairs with only 2 hurdles per player, these are great for improving short stepping lateral marking skills (*see* fig. 2.10c)

Key

Direction of run ⟶

Player

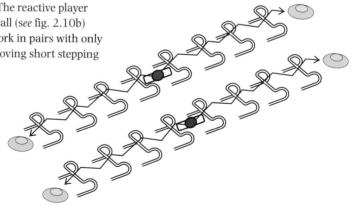

Figure 2.10(a) Mirror drills with hurdles

MIRROR DRILLS WITH HURDLES contd.

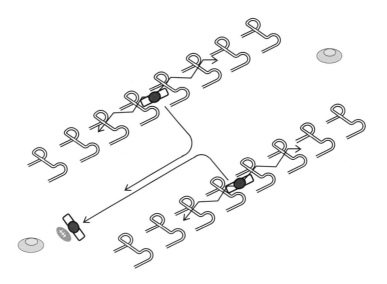

Figure 2.10(b) First-to-the-ball mirror drills

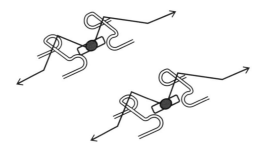

Figure 2.10(c) Short-stepping mirror drills

Key		
Direction of ball and run		⟶
Player		
Ball		

DRILL RUNNING FORM – COMPLEX MECHANICS

Aim

To prevent players from resorting to 'bad habits', particularly when under pressure. To challenge players by placing them in game-like pressure situations, and to maintain good running form even in the most difficult and demanding of situations.

Area/equipment

Indoor or outdoor area – hurdles. Place 4 hurdles in a straight line with 0.5-metre intervals between each hurdle. The next 4 hurdles are set slightly to one side and the final 4 hurdles are placed back in line with the original 4 (*see* fig. 2.11a).

Description

The player performs a dead-leg run over the hurdles, with the dead leg changing over the 4 centre hurdles. Return to the start by performing the drill over the hurdles in the opposite direction.

Key teaching points

- Maintain correct arm mechanics
- Work off the balls of the feet
- Try to develop and maintain a rhythm
- Keep eyes/head up and look forwards
- Maintain correct arm mechanics
- Maintain an upright posture
- Keep the hips square

Figure 2.11(a) Complex mechanic drills

Sets and reps

4 sets of 4 reps.

Variations/progressions

- Perform the drill laterally, moving both forwards and backwards to cross the centre 4 hurdles (*see* fig. 2.11b)
- Introduce the ball with short passes and ensure that players re-assert the correct arm mechanics after passing the ball back

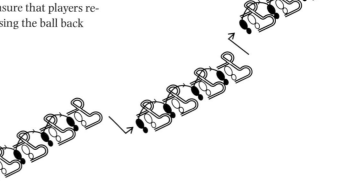

Key
Left foot
Right foot
Direction of movement ⟶

Figure 2.11(b) Complex lateral mechanic drills

CHAPTER 3 INNERVATION

THE DEVELOPMENT OF FAST FEET FOR RUGBY

This is the transition stage, from the warm-up and mechanics to periods of high intensity of work that activate the neural pathways. In other words, this stage gets the nerves to fire the muscles as quickly as possible. Using the Fast Foot Ladder, dance-like patterns such as twists, jumps and turns are all introduced. Rugby-specific footwork drills that require speed, co-ordination and agility such as side-step shuffles are practised explosively with and without the ball. The key here is to speed up the running techniques without compromising the quality of the mechanics. The innervation drills in this chapter progress from simple footwork patterns to complex rugby-specific drills, including ball and collision work.

DRILL   *FAST FOOT LADDER – SINGLE RUNS*

Aim
To develop fast feet with control, precision and power.

Area/equipment
Indoor or outdoor area – Fast Foot Ladder. Ensure that this is the correct ladder for the type of surface being used.

Description
The player covers the length of the ladder by placing one foot in each ladder space (*see* fig. 3.1a). Return to the start by jogging back on the outside of the ladder.

Key teaching points
- Maintain correct running form/mechanics
- Start slowly and gradually increase the speed
- Maintain an upright posture
- Stress that quality, not quantity, is important

Sets and reps
3 sets of 4 reps with 1 minute recovery between each set.

Variations/progressions
- Single lateral step – as above but performed laterally (*see* fig. 3.1b)
- 'In and out' – moving sideways along the ladder, stepping into and out of each ladder space, i.e. both feet in and both feet out (*see* fig. 3.1c)
- 'Icky shuffle' – side-stepping movement into and out of each ladder space while moving forwards (*see* fig. 3.1d)
- Double run – perform as single run but with both feet in each ladder space (*see* fig. 3.1e)
- Hopscotch – perform as double run above but with both feet outside the ladder on alternate spaces (*see* fig. 3.1f)
- Single-space jumps – two-footed jumps into and out of each ladder space (*see* fig. 3.1g)

FAST FOOT LADDER – SINGLE RUNS contd.

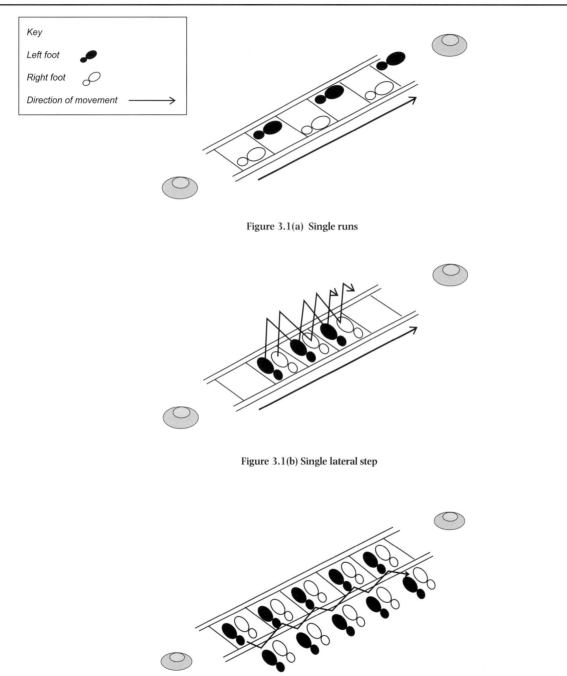

Key

Left foot

Right foot

Direction of movement

Figure 3.1(a) Single runs

Figure 3.1(b) Single lateral step

Figure 3.1(c) In-and-out

FAST FOOT LADDER – SINGLE RUNS contd.

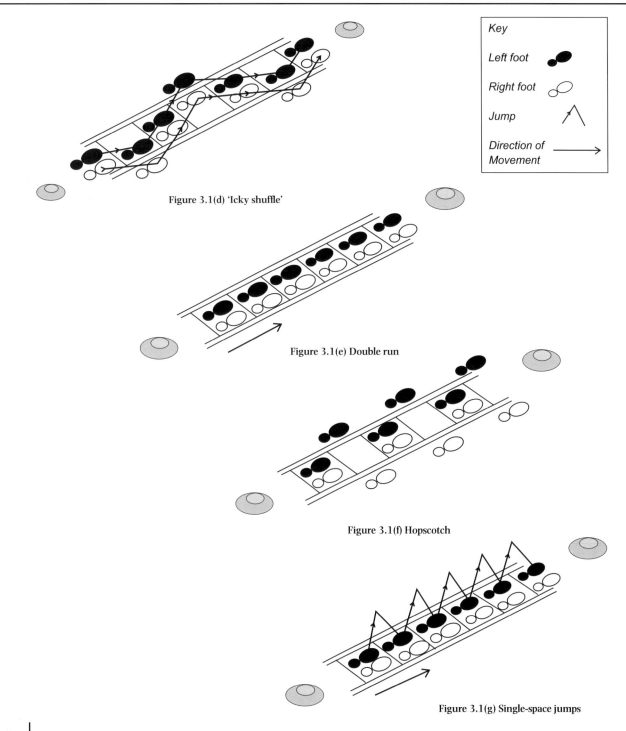

Key

Left foot

Right foot

Jump

Direction of Movement

Figure 3.1(d) 'Icky shuffle'

Figure 3.1(e) Double run

Figure 3.1(f) Hopscotch

Figure 3.1(g) Single-space jumps

DRILL FAST FOOT LADDER – 'T' FORMATION

Aim

To develop speed and control of acceleration when pressing/attacking the opposition. To develop controlled lateral pressing skills and co-ordinated backward movement prior to turning and chasing.

Area/equipment

Indoor or outdoor area. Place 2 ladders in a 'T' formation with a cone placed at the end of each ladder.

Description

The player accelerates down the ladder using single steps. On reaching the ladder crossing the end, the player moves laterally either left or right using short lateral steps. On coming out of the ladder the player then moves backwards in a side-on running motion, keeping both the eyes and head looking forwards.

Key teaching points

- Maintain correct running form/mechanics
- Encourage strong arm-drive when transferring from linear to lateral steps
- When moving backwards, keep the head and eyes up
- Do not skip backwards

Sets and reps

3 sets of 4 reps with 1 minute recovery between each set (2 moving to the left and 2 moving to the right).

Variations/progressions

- Start with a lateral run and upon reaching the end ladder accelerate in a straight line forwards down the ladder
- Mix and match previous Fast Foot Ladder drills (*see* pp. 53–55)
- Up, across and drive – place a ball and shield 2 metres away at both ends of the ladder (*see* fig. 3.2b)

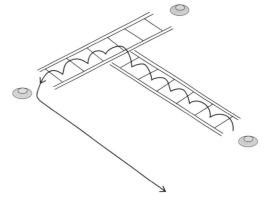

Figure 3.2(a) Fast Foot Ladder drill – up, across and backwards

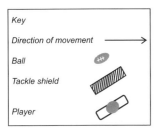

Key

Direction of movement →

Ball

Tackle shield

Player

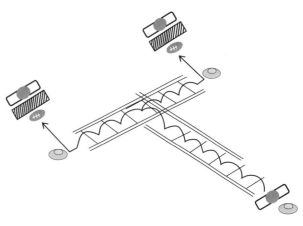

Figure 3.2(b) Up across and drive

55

DRILL   FAST FOOT LADDER – CROSSOVER

Aim

To develop speed, agility and change of direction in a more rugby-specific 'crowded' area. To improve reaction time, peripheral vision and timing.

Area/equipment

Large indoor or outdoor area. Place 4 ladders in a cross formation, leaving a clear centre space of approximately 3 square metres. Place a cone 1 metre from the start of each ladder.

Description

Split the squad into 4 equal groups and locate them at the start of each ladder – A, B, C and D (*see* fig. 3.3a). Players accelerate down the ladder simultaneously, performing a single-step drill. On reaching the end of the ladder, players accelerate across the centre square and onwards to join the end of the queue at the start of the ladder opposite them. Do not travel down this ladder.

Key teaching points

■ Maintain correct running form/mechanics
■ Keep the head and eyes up and be aware of other players, particularly around the centre area

Sets and reps

3 sets of 6 reps with 1 minute recovery between each set.

Variations/progressions

■ At the end of the first ladder, side-step to the right or left and single-step down the appropriate adjacent ladder (*see* fig. 3.3b)
■ Vary the Fast Foot Ladder drills performed down the first ladder
■ Include a 360° turn in the centre square; this is great for positional awareness
■ Practise collision work – place 4 shields and players in the centre area, approximately 1 metre away from the end of the ladders. At the end of the ladder the player hits and turns on the shield and then accelerates back to the adjacent ladder (*see* fig. 3.3c)

CROSSOVER DRILLS contd.

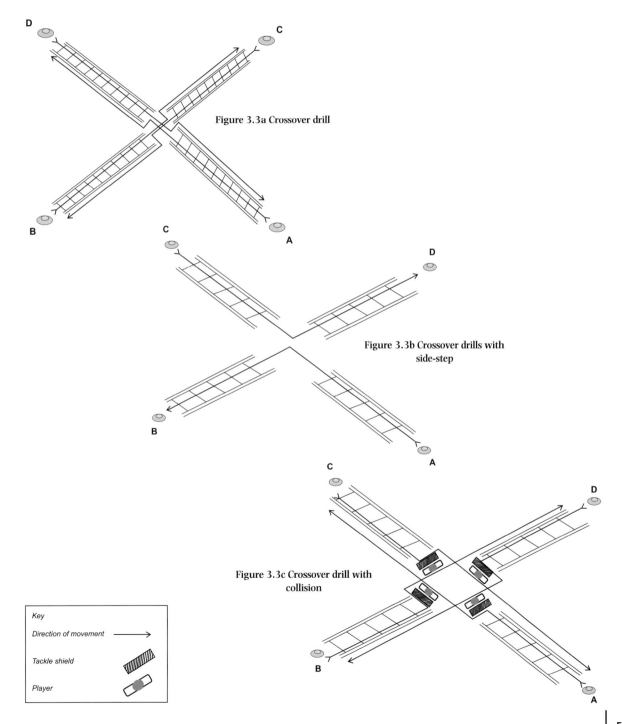

Figure 3.3a Crossover drill

Figure 3.3b Crossover drills with side-step

Figure 3.3c Crossover drill with collision

Key

Direction of movement

Tackle shield

Player

DRILL FAST FOOT LADDER – WITH A BALL

Aim
To develop fast feet, speed and agility while incorporating game specific ball control.

Area/equipment
Large indoor or outdoor area. Place a Fast Foot
Ladder with a cone at each end approximately 1
metre away.

Description
One player performs fast foot drills down the ladder,
either laterally or linearly. A second player –
standing 2 metres away from the ladder in a central
position – feeds the ball in to the player at different
heights, requiring the first player to catch, control
and return the ball.

Key teaching points
■ Concentrate on good footwork patterns
■ Ensure that correct technical skills are used when controlling and
  returning the ball
■ Ensure that the player performing the drill returns to correct
  running form/mechanics after returning the ball

Sets and reps
3 sets of 6 reps with 1 minute recovery between each set.

Variations/progressions
Vary the Fast Foot Ladder drills performed by the players (see pp.
  53–55).

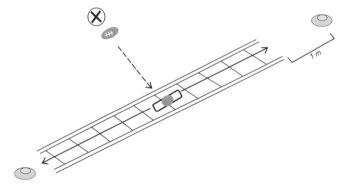

Figure 3.4 Fast feet drill with ball

| DRILL | *FAST FOOT LADDER – WITH PASSING* |

Aim

To develop fast feet and agility while incorporating rugby-specific ball control and passing combination drills.

Area/equipment

Large indoor or outdoor area. Place 2 ladders in an upside-down 'L' pattern, with 2 more mirroring these, approximately 2 metres away. Place cones at the start and end of each ladder (1 metre away). Place another 2 cones 15 metres away and 1 metre apart in line with the centre space. At the end of one ladder, place a ball.

Description

Two players start with linear fast foot drills then transfer to lateral drills as the ladders dictate. Player 1 accelerates on to the ball supplied by the coach. Player 1 then passes the ball across the grid to player 2, who on receiving the ball cuts inside and performs a switch movement with player 1 who receives the ball and straightens up.

Key teaching points

- Maintain correct running form/mechanics
- Ensure that correct technical skills are used when players are on the ball
- Encourage players to use clear communication – both visual and audio

Sets and reps

3 sets of 6 reps with 1 minute recovery between each set (i.e. 3 reps as player 1 and 3 reps as player 2.

Variations/progressions

- Vary the Fast Foot Ladder drills performed linearly and laterally by the players (*see* pp. 53–55.
- Introduce a dummy pass by player 2

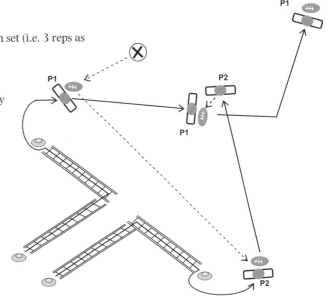

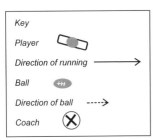

Figure 3.5 Fast feet with passing drill

DRILL FAST FOOT LADDER – CLOSE-CONTACT

Aim
To develop fast feet, agility and control in a restricted area while under pressure from other players.

Area/equipment
Large indoor or outdoor area – place 4 ladders side by side.

Description
Working in pairs, players work on each of the outside ladders and perform fast foot drills while covering the length of the ladder. On the coach's signal the players move to the centre ladders, thus working side by side (*see* fig. 3.6a).

Key teaching points
- Maintain correct running form/mechanics
- Encourage players to push and nudge each other to simulate the close-contact situations that occur in a game
- If players are 'knocked' off balance, ensure that they re-assert the correct arm mechanics as soon as possible
- On passing the ball, ensure that the player re-asserts the correct arm mechanics as soon as possible.

Sets and reps
3 sets of 4 reps with 1 minute recovery between each set.

Variations/progressions
- Start players from the centre ladders and work them out and back in
- Start players on ladders next to each other, on either the left or right of the grid, and work them across the 4 ladders (*see* fig. 3.6b)
- Introduce the ball with the players running with the ball in one arm
- Introduce short passes between the players
- Competition – place a ball on the ground in the centre area, 2 metres away from the end of the ladders. The players compete to secure the ball first

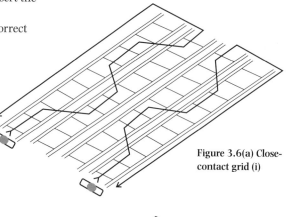

Figure 3.6(a) Close-contact grid (i)

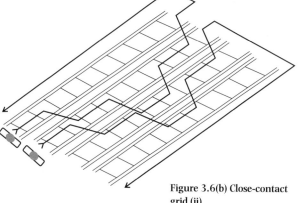

Figure 3.6(b) Close-contact grid (ii)

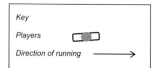

Key

Players

Direction of running

DRILL FAST FOOT LADDER – GIANT CROSSOVER

Aim
To develop fast feet, speed, agility, co-ordination and visual reaction skills, both with and without the ball.

Area/equipment
Large indoor or outdoor area. Place 4 ladders in a cross formation with 25 metres between the ladders in the centre area. Place a ball at the end of one ladder and another at the end of an adjacent ladder.

Description
Split the squad into 4 equal groups and locate them at the start of each ladder. Players accelerate simultaneously down the ladder, performing fast foot drills (*see* pp. 53–55). Two players will have a ball at the end of their respective ladders; the ball is passed to them as they accelerate across the centre area. The player who has received the ball then pop-passes the ball to the oncoming player. Well-timed passes mean the ball will remain in the centre area. Having passed the ball, the player runs to the start of the queue on the opposite side of the cross. Do not travel down this ladder.

Key teaching points
- Ensure drill is continuous
- Maintain correct running form/mechanics
- Ensure that correct technical skills are used when players are on the ball
- Encourage players to use clear communication

Sets and reps
3 sets of 6 reps with 1 minute recovery between each set.

Variations/progressions
- Vary the passing drills used in the centre area
- Vary the amount of control allowed, e.g. one touch, two touch, etc.

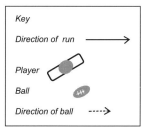

Figure 3.7 Giant crossover

DRILL FAST FOOT LADDER – LONG KICK/CATC

Aim
To develop fast feet, speed, agility and acceleration while focusing on getting into position early to receive a long kick in the air. To develop kicking over a long distance.

Area/equipment
Large indoor or outdoor area – 4 ladders. Place 2 ladders next to each other 10 metres apart. The other 2 ladders should be placed in the same formation 40–50 metres away from the first 2.

Description
Split the squad in to 4 equal groups and locate them at the ends of each ladder so that all players are facing the centre space. Players perform nominated fast foot drills down the ladders (*see* pp. 53–55). Two players will receive a ball and then punt the ball in a straight line to the players coming down the opposite ladders (*see* fig. 3.8a). On completing the kicks the players run backwards to the start position. On receiving the punted ball, this player repeats the drill.

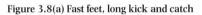

Figure 3.8(a) Fast feet, long kick and catch

Key teaching points
■ Maintain correct running form/mechanics
■ Ensure that correct technical skills are used when players are kicking and catching the ball
■ The timing of the player receiving the ball is crucial. He should receive the ball *just after he has left the ladder*
■ The player catching the ball must explode vertically to take the ball

Sets and reps
3 sets of 6 reps with 1 minute recovery between each set.

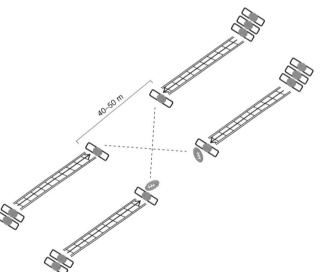

Figure 3.8(b) Fast-feet, long diagonal kick and catch

Variations/progressions
■ Make the long kick diagonally to the oncoming player on the adjacent ladder (*see* fig. 3.8b)
■ For sprint endurance conditioning make the players accelerate across the centre space to join the start of the ladder diagonally opposite them

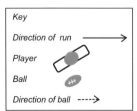

Key	
Direction of run	→
Player	
Ball	
Direction of ball	---->

DRILL FAST FOOT LADDER – SUPPORT THE PASS

Key

Direction of run ——————→

Player

Ball

Direction of ball ----→

Tackle bag ▨▨▨▨

Aim

To develop fast, controlled acceleration. To develop the ability to pass and control the ball in a restricted area and to change direction to support the player on the ball.

Area/equipment

Large indoor or outdoor area approximately 35 square metres – 7 ladders and balls. Place 3 ladders out in a straight line next to one another, 5 metres apart. Ten metres from the end of the first line of ladders the other 4 ladders are placed next to one another, 5 metres apart (*see* fig. 3.9a). Two players/coaches are located at the extreme left and right between 2 sets of ladders.

Description

Working in groups of 3 the players accelerate down the ladders in a slightly staggered formation: the player on the end-ladder out first; the player on the middle ladder second; and the player on the third ladder last. On coming out of the ladder the ball is transferred from one side to the other. On passing the ball the players side-step in to support the ball before accelerating down the second ladder.

Key teaching points

■ Maintain correct running form/mechanics
■ Do not present the hands too soon for the ball, as this will cause deceleration
■ Once the ball has been passed on, the players should be encouraged to re-assert the correct arm mechanics

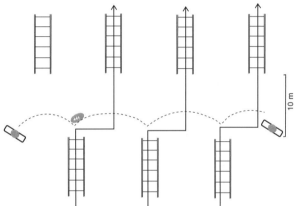

Figure 3.9(a) Fast hands support the pass

Sets and reps

3 sets of 5 reps with a walk-back recovery between each repetition and a 2-minute recovery between each set.

Variations/progressions

Introduce shields 3 metres away from the first 3 ladders. The player hits the shield, turns, passes the ball on then supports the player with the ball (*see* fig. 3.9b).

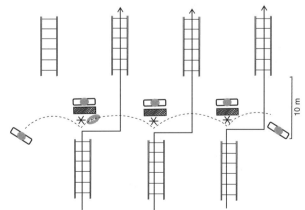

Figure 3.9(b) Fast hands support the pass with contact

DRILL   LINE DRILLS

Aim
To develop quickness of the feet.

Area/equipment
Indoor or outdoor area – use any line marked on the ground surface.

Description
The player performs single split-steps over the line and back – right foot forward, left foot back then right foot back, left foot forward.

Key teaching points
- Maintain good arm mechanics
- Maintain an upright posture
- Maintain a strong core
- Encourage development of a rhythm
- Keep the head and eyes up

Sets and reps
3 sets of 20 reps with 1 minute recovery between each set.

Variations/progressions
- Two-footed jumps over the line and back (*see* fig. 3.10b)
- Stand astride the line and bring the feet in to touch the line before sending them back out again. Perform the drill as quickly as possible (*see* fig. 3.10c)
- Two-footed side jumps over the line and back (*see* fig. 3.10d)
- Two-footed side jumps with a 180° twist in the air over the line and back (*see* fig. 3.10e)
- Complex variation – introduce the ball either at the end of the drill so that the player explodes on to it, or during the drill so that the player passes back before continuing with the drill

Always revert to good arm mechanics after passing the ball back

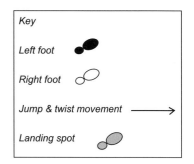

Key

Left foot

Right foot

Jump & twist movement

Landing spot

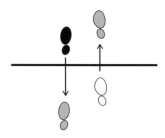

Figure 3.10(a) Single split-steps

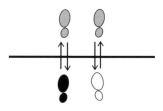

Figure 3.10(b) Two-footed jumps

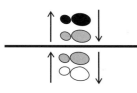

Figure 3.10(c) Astride jumps

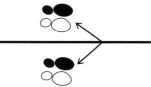

Figure 3.10(d) Two-footed side jumps over and back

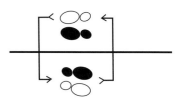

Figure 3.10(e) Two-footed side jumps with 180° twist

DRILL   *QUICK BOX-STEPS*

Aim
To develop explosive power and control. (**NB**: The emphasis is on speed.)

Area/equipment
Indoor or outdoor area – a strong box, bench or aerobics step with a non-slip surface approximately 30 cm in height.

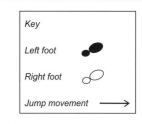

Description
The player performs an alternating split-step jump on the box, i.e. one foot on the box and one on the floor.

Key teaching points
- Practise the drill slowly first to perfect balance and foot placement, then build up speed
- Focus on good arm-drive
- Maintain an upright posture
- Maintain a strong core
- Keep the head and eyes up
- Work off the balls of the feet
- Work at a high level of intensity once technique is perfected
- Encourage development of a rhythm

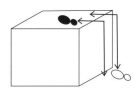

Figure 3.11(a) Alternating split step

Sets and reps
3 sets of 20 reps with 1 minute recovery between each set.

Variations/progressions
- Two-footed jumps on to and off of the box (*see* fig. 3.11b)
- Two-footed side jumps on to and off of the box (lead with the left shoulder for 10 reps and then the right shoulder for 10 reps)
- Straddle jumps on to and off of the box
- Single-footed hops on and off the box (lead with the left foot for 10 reps and then the right foot for 10 reps) (*see* fig. 3.11e)
- The ball can be introduced for quick, short passes
- Instead of using a normal rugby ball for passing, use a 3 kg Jelly Ball.

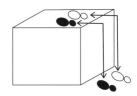

Figure 3.11(b) Two-footed jumps

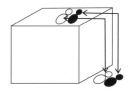

Figure 3.11(c) Two-footed side jumps

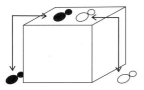

Figure 3.11(d) Straddle split-jumps

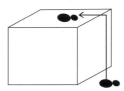

Figure 3.11(e) Single-footed hops

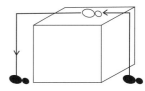

Figure 3.11(f) Double alternate single hop

CHAPTER 4 ACCUMULATION OF POTENTIAL

THE SAQ RUGBY CIRCUIT

This is the part of the continuum where we bring together those areas of work already practised. Many of the mechanics and fast feet drills are specific to developing a particular skill; in rugby, skills are not isolated but clustered. An example of this is when a player needs to run mechanically well for 30 metres, decelerate, move with fast feet to change direction, tackle, jump, turn, side-step and then stop and assess the situation. All this may occur over a varying period of time. Using ladders, hurdles, cones and poles, etc. rugby-specific circuits can be used to develop programmed agility as well as conditioning the player for this type of high-intensity work.

> Do not use this phase to fatigue the players but to challenge them with a variety of skills. Ensure that a maximum recovery period is implemented between sets and reps.

DRILL   AGILITY RUNS – 4-SQUARE BALL

Aim
To develop multi-directional explosive speed, turn mechanics and running mechanics both with and without the ball.

Area/equipment
Indoor or outdoor area of approximately 10 square metres – 5 cones are placed one on each corner and 1 in the middle. Rugby balls are placed in the centre around the cone.

Description
The player starts at the centre cone (E), grabs a ball and accelerates to cone (A) where the ball is placed on the cone. The player then returns to the centre cone and picks up another ball, accelerates to cone (B) and places the ball on the cone. The drill is completed when the final ball has been placed on cone (D) and the player has accelerated to finish at the centre cone (*see* fig. 4.1).

Key teaching points
- Maintain correct running form/mechanics
- Encourage strong arm mechanics both with and without the ball
- Do not allow the feet to cross over on the turn
- Encourage players to return upright as soon as possible after picking up the ball
- Use short steps and work off the balls of the feet at all times

Sets and reps
5 reps with a 2-minute recovery between each rep.

Variations/progressions
Players have to go around the corner cones.

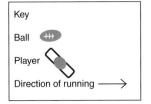

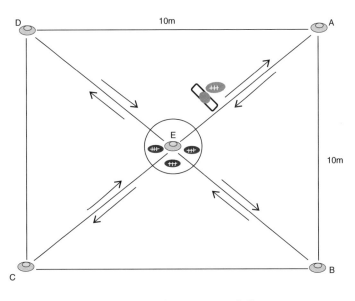

Figure 4.1 Agility run – square ball

DRILL AGILITY RUNS – 'T'-RUN

Aim
To develop rugby-specific speed and agility.

Area/equipment
Indoor or outdoor area – 4 poles or cones. Place the poles or cones out in a 'T' formation (*see* fig. 4.2a), 5 metres apart.

Description
The player starts on the left-hand side of the first pole and accelerates to the pole directly ahead. He then passes around this pole and turns to his right before accelerating on to the end pole. The player then runs around the end pole and returns to the middle pole before finishing on the opposite side at the start position (*see* fig. 4.2a). Repeat the drill by starting on the right of the first pole and turn to the left at the middle pole.

Key teaching points
- Maintain correct running form/mechanics
- Work on shortening the steps used in the turn
- Focus on increasing the speed of the arm-drive when coming out of the turns
- Ensure players work their weak sides (most players will have a preferred turning side)

Sets and reps
3 sets of 5 reps with a 30-second recovery between each rep and 1 minute recovery between each set.

Variations/progressions
The coach stands at the centre cone. The player accelerates towards the coach, who provides a signal – verbal or visual – to dictate which way the player turns.

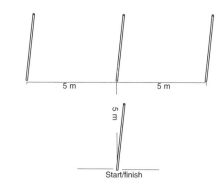

Figure 4.2(a) T-run grid

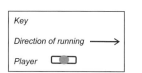

Key

Direction of running ⟶

Player

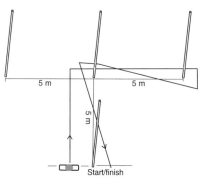

Figure 4.2(b) T-run right

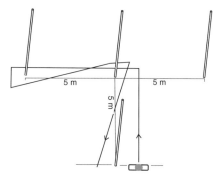

Figure 4.2(c) T-run left

DRILL AGILITY RUNS – SWERVE DEVELOPMENT

Aim

To develop fine angle running at pace, as if trying to penetrate the defensive line or explode into a gap.

Area/equipment

A large indoor or outdoor area. 8–12 poles or cones set out in a 'zig-zag' formation (*see* fig. 4.3). The distances between the poles or cones should be 2–4 metres at varying angles (this will make the runs more realistic). The total length of the run will be 25–30 metres.

Description

The player accelerates from the first cone and swerves in and around all of the others before completing the course. The player gently jogs back to the starting cone before repeating the drill.

Key teaching points

- Maintain correct running form/mechanics
- Work on shortening the steps used in the turn
- Focus on increasing speed of the arm-drive when coming out of the turns
- Ensure players do not take wide angles around the cones
- Keep the head and eyes up

Sets and reps

3 sets of 5 reps with a 30-second recovery between each rep and 1 minute recovery between each set.

Variations/progressions

Use light hand weights for the first 4 reps then perform the last rep without the weights as a contrast.

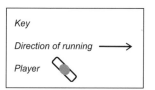

Key

Direction of running $\longrightarrow$

Player

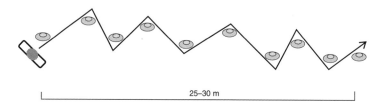

25–30 m

Figure 4.3 Swerve-development runs

DRILL   AGILITY RUNS – ZIG-ZAG

Aim
To develop fast, controlled and angled lateral runs.

Area/equipment
Indoor or outdoor area. Mark out a grid using 10–12 cones or poles in 2 lines of 5–6. Stagger the obstacles so that the line makes a zig-zag formation (*see* fig. 4.4a).

Description
The player runs the zig-zag formation staying on the inside of the cones or poles, and then walks back to the start before repeating the drill.

Key teaching points
- Maintain correct running form/mechanics
- Players must keep their hips facing the direction in which they are running
- Encourage players to use short steps
- Ensure players do not skip
- Ensure players use good arm mechanics

Sets and reps
3 sets of 6 reps with a walk-back recovery between each rep and 1 minute recovery between each set.

Variations/progressions
- Perform the drill backwards, with a side-stepping movement
- Players go *around* each cone rather than staying on the inside of them
- 'Up and back' – enter the grid sideways and move forwards to the first cone then backwards to the next, etc.
- Add a Fast Foot Ladder to the start and finish for acceleration and deceleration running (*see* fig. 4.4b)

> Arm mechanics are as vital in lateral movements as they are in linear movements. Many players forget to use their arms when they are moving sideways.

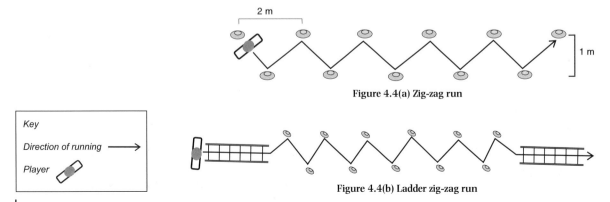

Figure 4.4(a) Zig-zag run

Key
Direction of running ⟶
Player

Figure 4.4(b) Ladder zig-zag run

DRILL AGILITY RUNS – ZIG-ZAG PICK-UP/PLACE

Aim
To develop fast, controlled and angled runs, with and without the ball. To practise picking the ball up from the side.

Area/equipment
Indoor or outdoor area. Mark out a grid using 10–12 cones or poles in 2 lines of 5-6. Stagger the obstacles so that the line makes a zig-zag formation (*see* fig. 4.5). On one side place 6 balls on the far side of the cones.

Description
The player runs the zig-zag formation, stepping over both the cone and the ball before picking the ball up, moving back across the grid and placing the ball at the cone on the opposite side of the grid. This is repeated until all the balls have been moved from one side of the grid to the other.

Key teaching points
- Use strong arm mechanics
- Keep the spine as straight as possible when squatting to pick the ball up and place it down
- Keep the head up
- Work off the balls of the feet
- Ensure that players re-assert good arm mechanics on the way up after placing down and picking up the ball

Sets and reps
5 reps with a 2-minute recovery between each set

Variations/progressions
- On one side of the grid use shields for the players to step over
- Players can perform the drill backwards
- Add a Fast Foot Ladder at the beginning and end

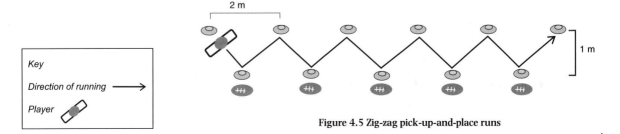

Figure 4.5 Zig-zag pick-up-and-place runs

DRILL   SAQ – RUGBY-SPECIFIC RUNS

Aim
To develop a creative range of rugby-specific running patterns likely to be encountered in games in order to enhance the players' skill base and keep them motivated and challenged.

Area/equipment
Half a rugby pitch – cones, hurdles, Fast Foot Ladders, poles, shields, tackle bags and rugby balls, all to be placed in a circuit within the area.

Description
The players follow a circuit which will take them through ladders, side-stepping and jumping over hurdles, side-stepping through cones, running backwards, jumping, turning, hitting shields, stepping over bags, receiving and sending passes. One circuit should take players 30–60 seconds to complete.

Key teaching points
■ Maintain correct running form/mechanics for all activities.

Sets and reps
1 set of 6 reps with a varied recovery time between each rep depending on the stage in the season.

Variations/progressions
The coach to use their imagination to add/subtract and vary the drills within the circuit. This will keep players motivated and challenged.

SAQ – RUGBY-SPECIFIC RUNS contd.

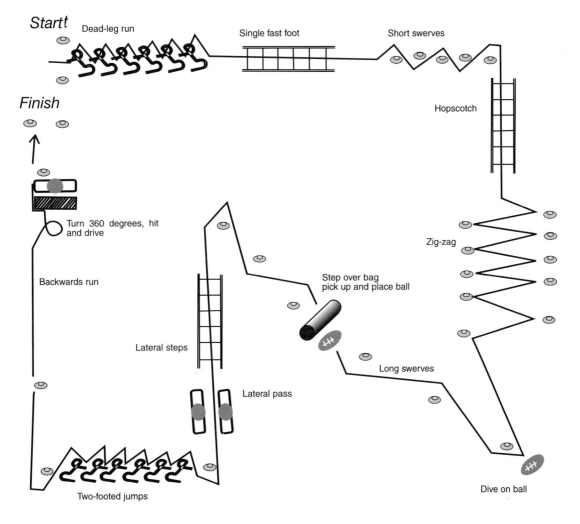

Figure 4.6 Rugby-specific runs

CHAPTER 5 EXPLOSION

3-STEP MULTI-DIRECTIONAL ACCELERATION FOR RUGBY

The exercises outlined in this chapter have been designed to boost response-times and develop multi-directional, explosive movements.

Programmable and random agility is trained using resisted and assisted high-quality plyometrics. Plyometric exercises focus on the stretch shortening cycle of the muscles involved, an action that is a central part of rugby performance. Plyometric drills include drop jumps, hops, skips and bounds. Plyometrics can be fun and challenging and also adds variety to training sessions. However, there is potential for injury with these exercises so they must be performed using the correct technique and at the correct point in the training session. Upper-body speed and power is also catered for with Jelly Ball workouts, great for the type of strength required to hold off an opponent.

The crucial element in using explosive drills is the implementation of the 'contrast phase'. This simply means performing the drill without resistance for one or two reps immediately after performing them with resistance. These movements will naturally be more explosive and more easily remembered and reproduced over a period of time. The key is to ensure that quality is the priority, not quantity. Efforts must be carefully monitored.

> This is a time for high-intensity explosive action, not 'tongue-hanging out fatigue'!

DRILL   *SEATED FORWARD GET-UPS*

Aim
To develop multi-directional explosive acceleration. To improve a player's ability to get up and accelerate all in one movement.

Area/equipment
Indoor or outdoor area of 20 square metres.

Description
The player sits on the floor facing the direction in which he is going to run and with his legs out straight in front of him. On a signal from the coach the player gets up as quickly as possible, accelerates for 10 metres and then slows down before jogging gently back to the start position.

Key teaching points
- Players should be encouraged to complete the drill in one smooth action
- Promote correct running form/mechanics
- Do not allow the players to get up, stop and then start to run
- Encourage players to get into an upright position and to drive the arms as soon as possible
- Ensure that the initial steps are short and powerful
- Do not encourage over-striding

Sets and reps
3 sets of 5 reps with a jog-back recovery between each rep and a 2-minute recovery between each set.

Variations/progressions
- Seated backward get-ups, turning to run forwards
- Seated sideways get-ups, turning to run forwards
- Lying get-ups (from the front, back, left and right)
- Kneeling get-ups
- Work in pairs and have get-up competitions – e.g. first to dive on the ball
- Work in pairs with 1 player in front of the other and perform 'tag' get-ups

DRILL   FLEXI-CORD – BUGGY RUNS

Aim
To develop multi-directional explosive acceleration.

Area/equipment
Indoor or outdoor area – place 3 cones in a line with 10 metres between each. Ensure that there is plenty of room for safe deceleration. 1 Viper Belt with a Flexi-cord attached at both ends by 2 anchor points.

Description
Working in pairs, player 1 wears the belt while player 2 stands behind holding the flexi-cord with his hands looped in and over it (this is for safety purposes). Player 2 allows the Flexi-cord to resist as player 1 accelerates forwards then runs behind at a distance sufficient to maintain a constant resistance over the first 10 metres. Both players need to decelerate over the second 10 metres. Player 1 removes the belt after the required number of reps and completes a contrast run on his own. Repeat the drill but swap roles.

Key teaching points
■ Player 1 must focus on correct running form/mechanics and explosive drive
■ Player 2 works *with* player 1 not against him, allowing the Flexi-cord to provide the resistance

Sets and reps
1 set of 6 reps plus 1 contrast run, with a 30-second recovery between each rep and a 3-minute recovery before the next drill.

Variations/progressions
■ Lateral buggy run – player 1 accelerates laterally for the first 2 metres before turning to cover the remaining distance linearly
■ After the acceleration phase of the contrast run, the coach can introduce a ball for the player to catch, control and drive forwards (*see* fig. 5.1)

Key	
Player	▭▬▭
Direction of running	⟶
Looped flexi cord	O
Ball	⬬

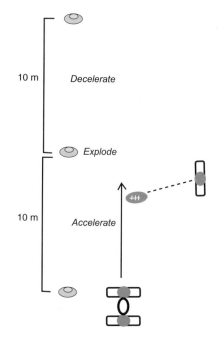

Figure 5.1 Flexi-cord resistance drill – buggy run with pass

10 m   *Decelerate*

Explode

10 m   *Accelerate*

DRILL FLEXI-CORD – OUT AND BACK

Aim

To develop short, explosive, angled acceleration runs – ideal for beating an opponent to the ball or into a space.

Area/equipment

Large indoor or outdoor area of 10 square metres – 5 cones to be positioned as shown in fig. 5.2. 1 Viper Belt with a Flexi-cord attached to only one anchor point on the belt and a safety belt on the other end of the Flexi-cord.

Description

Working in pairs, player 1 wears the Viper Belt. Player 2 stands directly behind player 1, holding the Flexi-cord and wearing the safety belt. The Flexi-cord should be taut prior to the drill commencing. Player 2 nominates a cone for player 1 to run out to, varying the calls between the 3 cones for the required number of repetitions. When player 1 arrives at the nominated cone a coach or a third player delivers a ball for player 1 to catch, control and pass back before they return to the start gate using short, sharp steps. Repeat for the prescribed number of reps, and finish with a contrast run before swapping roles.

Key teaching points

- Focus on short, sharp explosive steps and a fast, powerful arm-drive
- Maintain correct running form/mechanics
- Work off the balls of the feet
- Use short steps while returning to the start to help develop balance and control

Sets and reps

3 sets of 6 reps plus 1 contrast run per set with a 3-minute recovery between each set. For advanced players, depending on the time of the season, increase to 9 reps.

Variations/progressions

- Perform the drill laterally
- Work backwards with short, sharp steps
- Have a player with a shield who randomly moves from cone to cone; the resisted player drives out to tackle the shield and so on

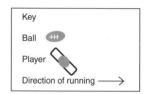

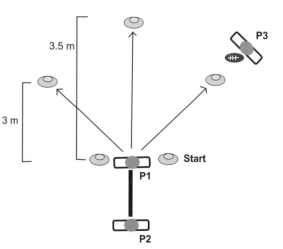

Figure 5.2 Flexi-cord resistance – out and back

DRILL FLEXI-CORD – WITH A LATERAL PASS

Aim
To develop explosive acceleration on to the ball, control and passing of the ball at speed and under pressure.

Area/equipment
Indoor or outdoor area – 4 cones set up in a square (3 m x 3m), 1 Viper Belt and a rugby ball.

Description
Player 1 and player 2 are connected by the Viper Belt and player 1 stands between the start cones marked A. Players 3 and 4 stand outside the cones marked B with player 3 holding a ball. Player 1 accelerates towards the gap between cones B and receives a pass from player 3 which he then transfers to player 4. Player 1 then jockeys backwards to the start position before repeating the drill. Vary the side of the grid that the ball is passed from.

Key teaching points
- Having passed the ball, player 1 should re-assert the correct arm mechanics as quickly as possible
- Maintain correct running form/mechanics
- Player 1 must not run with arms out waiting for the pass, as this will cause deceleration

Sets and reps
2 sets of 10 reps plus 2 contrast runs, with the jockey backwards as the recovery between reps and a 3-minute recovery between each set.

Variations/progressions
- Vary the type of pass – high, low, etc.

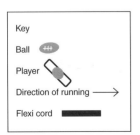

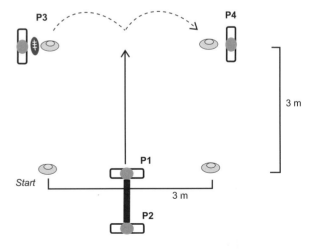

Figure 5.3 Flexi-cord resistance – out-and-back with lateral pass

DRILL FLEXI-CORD – BALL-HANDLING WORK

Aim
To develop explosive, controlled and powerful lateral movements. To improve hand–eye co-ordination and passing skills while moving laterally.

Area/equipment
Indoor or outdoor area – 4 cones placed in 2 sets of 2 to mark 2 start points and a ball (*see* fig. 5.4). 2 sets of Viper Belts with 4 Flexi-cords, one attached to each side.

Description
Working in 2 groups of 3 players, player 1 wears the Viper Belt. Players 2 and 3 stand one on each side of player 1 holding the Flexi-cord. The two groups face each other approximately 3 metres apart. On the coach's signal the resisted players move from left to right, passing the ball between them.

Key teaching points
- Work off the balls of the feet – do not skip sideways
- Maintain correct lateral running form/mechanics
- Push off with the back foot, do not pull with the front foot
- Re-assert arm mechanics as soon as the ball is passed

Sets and reps
2 sets of 10 reps (5 to the left and 5 to the right) plus 2 contrast runs per set (1 to the left and 1 to the right), with a 3-minute recovery between each set.

Variations/progressions
Turn the players so they are side-on to each other. They perform lateral passes while moving backwards and forwards.

> Although it is unusual to pass the ball while running backwards, when a player is tackled and driven backwards they may attempt to offload the ball in this pressured situation to keep the game alive.

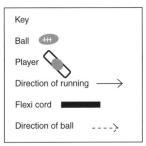

Key

Ball

Player

Direction of running ⟶

Flexi cord

Direction of ball ---->

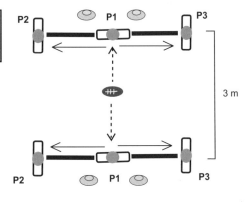

Figure 5.4 Flexi-cord resistance ball-handling work

DRILL FLEXI-CORD – VERTICAL EXPLOSIVE POWER

Aim

To develop vertical take-off power for the production of more air-time and height when jumping to catch a line-out ball or a high ball during open play.

Area/equipment

Indoor or outdoor area – approximately 3–4 square metres. 1 Viper Belt with 2 Flexi-cords and 1 ball.

Description

Working in groups of 4, 1 player wears the Viper Belt which has 2 Flexi-cords attached – one on either side of the belt (*see* photo). 2 other players stand a metre away, one either side of the resisted player, and stand on the Flexi-cord with their legs approximately 1 metre apart. The fourth player stands in front of the resisted player, holding the ball above their head; the resisted player then jumps to grab the ball, lands, passes the ball back to the fourth player and prepares himself to repeat the drill.

Key teaching points

- Do not sink into the hips either before take-off or on landing
- Work off the balls of the feet
- On landing, regain balance and prepare before the next jump
- Maintain correct jumping form/mechanics for each rep

Sets and reps

3 sets of 8 reps plus 1 contrast jump, with a 3-minute recovery between each set.

Variations/progressions

- Quick jumps – i.e. no setting between jumps. These are fast, repetitive jumps performed as quickly as possible
- Hold a rugby ball above the resisted player who has to jump and grab the ball. On landing the player passes the ball back for the drill to continue

DRILL FLEXI-CORD – RESISTED HIT

Aim
To develop explosive get-up and acceleration into the tackle.

Area/equipment
Outdoor area –1 Viper Belt and a tackle shield.

Description
Player 1 wears the Viper Belt and player 2 provides the resistance from behind. Player 3 holds the shield a stride-length away from player 1, who commences each drill from a prone position. Player 1 explodes from the ground and hits the shield back for approximately 1 m before returning to the prone position. Player 2 takes a stride forwards for each hit to maintain a constant resistance.

Key teaching points
- Player 1 must use an explosive arm-drive during the get-up and acceleration phases of the drill, and short explosive steps
- Player 3 must ensure that the shield is held at an angle over player 1

Sets and reps
1 set of 10 reps plus 2 contrast reps per set, with the drop to the ground as the recovery between reps and a 3-minute recovery before the next drill.

Variations/progressions
Player 3 can hold the shield to the left, centre and right to vary the angle and direction of player 1's hit.

DRILL FLEXI-CORD – OVERSPEED

Aim
To develop lightning quick acceleration.

Area/equipment
Indoor or outdoor area – 4 cones and 1 Viper Belt with a Flexi-cord. Place the cones out in a 'T' formation with 3 metres between each cone (*see* fig. 5.5).

Description
Working in pairs, player 1 wears the Viper Belt and faces player 2 who holds the Flexi-cord and has the safety belt around his waist – i.e the Flexi-cord will go from belly button to belly button. Player 1 stands at the cone marked A; player 2 stands at the cone marked B and walks backwards and away from player 1 thereby increasing the Flexi-cord resistance. After stretching the Flexi-cord for 4–5 metres, player 1 accelerates towards player 2 who then nominates either cone C or D, requiring player 1 to explosively change direction. Both players walk back to the start and repeat the drill.

Key teaching points
- Maintain correct running form/mechanics
- Control the running form/mechanics
- During the change-of-direction phase, shorten the steps and increase the rate of firing the arms

Sets and reps
3 sets of 8 reps plus 1 contrast run with a 3-minute recovery between each set.

Variations/progressions
- Player 1 starts with a horizontal jump before accelerating away
- Introduce the ball for the player to run on to after the change-of-direction phase
- Introduce a support player who works behind the assisted player and presents the ball to the support player on the assisted change-of-direction phase

Key	
Player	▭▬▭
Direction of running	⟶
Flexi cord	▬▬▬

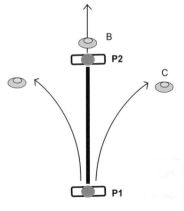

Figure 5.5 Flexi-cord drills – overspeed

DRILL   SIDE-STEPPER – RESISTED LATERAL RUNS

Aim
To develop explosive, controlled lateral patterns of running.

Area/equipment
Indoor or outdoor area – 10–12 cones placed in a zig-zag pattern (*see* fig. 5.6) and a Side-Stepper.

Description
The player wearing the Side-Stepper covers the length of the grid by running a lateral zig-zag pattern between the cones. Just before arriving at the cone, he extends the last step to increase the level of resistance. On completing a run, he turns around and works back along the grid.

Key teaching points
- Maintain correct lateral running form/mechanics
- Do not sink into the hips when stepping off to change direction
- During the directional change phase, increase arm-speed to provide additional control

Sets and reps
3 sets of 6 reps plus 1 contrast run with no recovery time between each rep and a 3-minutes recovery between each set.

Variations/progressions
- Perform the drill backwards
- Include the ball for short, fast passing

Key

Direction of running ⟶

Player

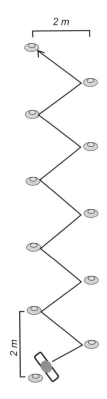

Figure 5.6 Side-Stepper Drills – resisted lateral runs

DRILL   SIDE-STEPPER – JOCKEYING IN PAIRS

Aim
To develop man-to-man marking skills with particular focus on defensive and attacking movement skills.

Area/equipment
Indoor or outdoor area – 6–8 cones. Mark out a channel approximately 20 metres long and 3 metres wide.

Description
Wearing a Side-Stepper, both players should face each other with approximately 2 metres between them. The attacking player moves from right to left in a backwards pattern, while the defending player attempts to mirror their movements to prevent the attacking player from having too much space. That is, the attacking player works in a forward direction and the defending player works backwards.

Key teaching points
■ Use quick low steps, *not* high knees
■ No skipping or jumping – 1 foot should be in contact with the floor at all times.
■ Try to keep the feet shoulder-width apart
■ Use a powerful arm-drive
■ Do not sink into the hips

Sets and reps
Sets of 4 reps, perform 1 set of 4 reps plus 1 or 2 contrast runs with a 30-second recovery between each rep and a 2-minute recovery between each set.

Variations/progressions
■ Both players perform the drill laterally, with one player leading and the other trying to mirror their movements
■ Introduce a tackle at the end of the grid with the defending player (2) initiating a tackle on the attacking player (1)

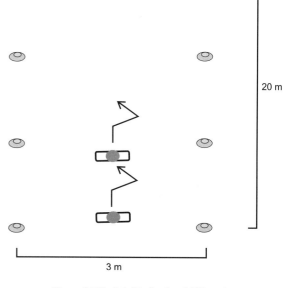

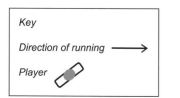

Key

Direction of running ⟶

Player

Figure 5.7 Resisted jockeying drill in pairs

DRILL *HAND-WEIGHT DROPS*

Aim
To develop explosive power, re-acceleration and specifically a powerful arm-drive.

Area/equipment
Indoor or outdoor area – 3 cones, hand weights of 1–2 kg. Place 1 cone down to represent the start, a second cone 15 metres away and the final cone 10 metres away from the second.

Description
Holding the weights, the player accelerates to the second cone, where he releases the hand weights keeping a natural flow to the arm mechanics. He continues to accelerate to the third cone before decelerating and walking back to the start to repeat the drill.

Key teaching points
- Maintain correct running form/mechanics
- Do not stop the arm-drive to release the weights
- Keep the head tall
- Quality not quantity is vital

Sets and reps
3 sets of 4 reps with a 3-minute recovery between each set.

Variations/progressions
- On the release of the hand-weights, the coach calls for a change of direction (i.e. the player is to accelerate off at different angles)
- Perform the drill backwards over the first 15 metres then turn, accelerate and release the weights to explode away
- Perform the drill laterally over the first 15 metres then turn, accelerate and release the weights to explode away

DRILL CONTACT TWIST AND ACCELERATION

Aim

To develop a powerful 'hit' in the contact phase and an explosive twist to get away from the tackler into the gap behind.

Area/equipment

Indoor or outdoor area – 3 cones, hand weights of 1–2 kg and 1 shield per group. Place 1 cone down to represent the start, a second cone 15 metres away and the final cone 5 metres away from the second (*see* fig. 5.8).

Description

Holding the weights, the player accelerates towards the second cone where the shield is situated. The player releases the hand weights 2 metres before the second cone, hits the shield, turns 360° and accelerates into the gap behind the shield before walking back to the start and repeating the drill.

Key teaching points

- Maintain correct running form/mechanics
- Do not stop the arm-drive to release the weights
- Keep the head tall
- Use short, explosive steps during the contact and turning phases
- Do not allow the feet to cross over
- Quality not quantity is vital

Sets and reps

1 or 2 sets of 5 reps with a walk-back recovery between each rep and a 3-minute recovery between each set.

Variations/progressions

- As the player accelerates into the gap behind the shield, a ball is passed for the player to explode on to

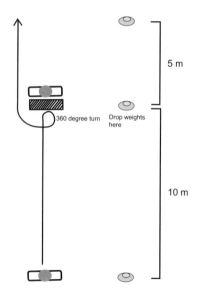

Figure 5.8 Hand-weight drops with contact twist and acceleration

5 m

360 degree turn   Drop weights here

10 m

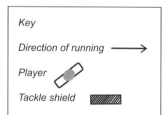

Key

Direction of running ⟶

Player

Tackle shield

DRILL *PARACHUTE RUNNING*

Aim
To develop explosive running over longer distances (sprint endurance) and explosive acceleration.

Area/equipment
Indoor or outdoor area – 4 cones and a parachute. Mark out a grid of 50 metres in length. Place 1 cone down as a start marker, 1 at a distance of 30 metres, 1 at 40 metres and 1 at 50 metres from the start marker.

Description
A player wearing the parachute accelerates to the cone 40 metres away then decelerates.

Key teaching points
- Maintain correct running form/mechanics
- Players may feel that they are being pulled from side to side. Reassure players that this will improve balance and co-ordination
- Do not over lean into the run
- Quality is vital, not quantity

Sets and reps
3 sets of 5 reps plus 1 contrast run, with a walk-back recovery between each rep and a 3-minute recovery between each set.

Variations/progressions
- Explosive re-acceleration – the parachutes have a release mechanism. The player accelerates to the 30-metre cone where he releases the parachute and explodes to the 40-metre cone before decelerating
- Random change of direction – the coach stands behind the 30-metre cone. As the player releases the parachute the coach indicates a change in the direction of the run. When mastered, the coach can then introduce the ball for players to run on to during the explosive phase.
- Collision work can also be practised here. Just after the release phase the player lowers the body and explodes into a tackle bag. (**NB**: The correct tackle technique is crucial here – head up, spine straight and attack horizontally)

DRILL   BALL DROPS

Aim
To develop explosive reactions.

Area/equipment
Indoor or outdoor area – 1 or 2 tennis balls or a plastic ball (size 4).

Description
Working in pairs, 1 player drops the ball at various distances and angles from his partner. The ball is dropped from shoulder height and immediately player 2 explodes forwards and attempts to catch or dive on the ball before the second bounce. (Distances between players will differ because the height of the bounce will vary depending on the ground surface.)

Key teaching points
- Work off the balls of the feet – particularly prior to the drop
- Use a very explosive arm-drive
- The initial steps should be short, fast and explosive
- At the take-off do not jump, stutter or hesitate
- Work on developing a smooth, one-movement run

Sets and reps
3 sets of 10 reps with a 2-minute recovery between each set.

Variations/progressions
- Player 1 to hold 2 balls and to drop just 1 in order that player 2 anticipates and selectively reacts to 1 ball only
- Working in groups of 3 with 2 of the players at different angles, alternately dropping a ball for the third player to catch or dive on. On achieving this, the player turns and accelerates away to catch/dive on the second ball
- Alter the start positions, e.g. sideways, backwards with a call, seated, etc.

DRILL   *UPHILL RUNS*

Aim
To develop sprint endurance and explosive running.

Area/equipment
Outdoors – the hill should be approximately 20–40 metres in length with a gradient of no more than 4%. A few cones can be used to mark out various distances.

Description
Players accelerate up the hill over a nominated distance and perform a slow jog-back to the start position before repeating the drill.

Key teaching points
- Maintain correct running form/mechanics
- Ensure that a strong knee- and arm-drive are used
- Work at maximal effort
- Adequate recovery time between reps is essential
- Do not attempt to run up hills with steep gradients, as this will have a negative impact on running mechanics

Sets and reps
3 sets of 6 reps with a jog-back recovery between reps and a 3-minute recovery between sets.

Variations/progressions
- Accelerate backward over the initial few metres before turning to complete the drill as above
- Overspeed – accelerate down the hill. (**NB:** Control is vital!)

DRILL BREAK-AWAY MIRROR DRILLS

Aim
To develop multi-directional explosive reactions.

Area/equipment
Indoor or outdoor area – 1 Break-Away Belt.

Description
Players work in pairs and face each other attached by the Break-Away Belt. Player 1 is the proactive player, while player 2 is reactive. Player 1 attempts to get away from player 2 by using either sideways, forward or backward movements. Players are not allowed to turn around and 'run away'. The drill ends if and when the proactive player breaks the reaction belt or the time limit runs out.

Key teaching points
- Stay focused on your partner
- Do not sink into the hips
- Keep the head tall and the spine straight
- Maintain correct arm mechanics

Sets and reps
3 sets where 1 set = 30 seconds of each player taking the proactive role followed by a recovery period of 1 minute.

Variations/progressions
- Side-by-side mirror drills – the object is for the proactive player to move away laterally and gain as much distance as possible before the reactive player can react.

DRILL — MEDICINE BALL (JELLY BALL) WORKOUT

Aim
To develop explosive upper-body and core power.

Area/equipment
Indoor or outdoor area – Jelly Balls or medicine balls of various weights from 3–8 kg.

Description
Working in pairs, the players perform simple throws standing roughly 2 metres apart, e.g. chest passes, single-arm passes, front slams, back slams, twist passes, woodchopper and granny throws (*see* photos).

Key teaching points
- Start with a lighter ball as a warm-up set
- Begin with simple movements first before progressing to twists, etc.
- Keep the spine in an upright position
- Take care when loading (catching) and unloading (throwing) as this can put stress on the lower back

Sets and reps
1 set of 12 reps of each drill, with a 1-minute recovery between each drill and 3 minutes before the next exercise.

Variations/progressions
Long passes – start by performing the pass with a rugby ball, then throw a Jelly Ball for 6 reps before performing a contrast pass with a light foam/plastic ball and then with a rugby ball.

DRILL JELLY BALL – TACKLE DEVELOPMENT

Aim
To develop an explosive hip/core thrust used when tackling.

Area/equipment
Indoor or outdoor area – 5, 6, 7 or 8 kg Jelly Balls may be used.

Description
Players can work on their own against a wall or with a partner. The player kneels down and leans slightly back, with the fingers cupped behind the ball at chest level. The player then thrusts the hips up and forwards and then throws the ball forwards.

Key teaching points
- The hip thrust is administered fractionally before the throw is performed
- Ensure that the player's hands/fingers are cupped behind the ball

Sets and reps
3 sets of 20 reps plus 2 contrast reps without the Jelly Ball, with a 2-minute recovery between each set.

Variations/progressions
Use 2, 3 or 4 kg Jelly Balls, i.e. 1 in each hand. This will provide additional proprioceptive training.

DRILL | *SPRINT SLED RUNNING*

Aim
To develop explosive sprint endurance.

Area/equipment
Large outdoor grass area – cones and a Sprint Sled. Mark out an area of 30–60 metres.

Description
The player is connected to the Sled and sprints over the nominated distance before recovering, turning around and repeating the drill.

Key teaching points
- Maintain correct running form/mechanics
- Maintain a strong arm drive
- Players will often need to use an exaggerated lean to initiate the momentum required to get the Sled moving
- As momentum picks up, the player should transfer into the correct running position

Sets and reps
2 sets of 5 reps plus 1 contrast run, with a 1-minute recovery between each rep and a 3-minute recovery between each set.

Variations/progressions
5-metre explosive acceleration – the player covers 50 metres by alternating between acceleration and deceleration phases over distances of 5 metres. (**NB**: Quality and not quantity work is the key here!)

DRILL PLYOMETRICS – LOW-IMPACT QUICK JUMPS

Aim
To develop explosive power for running, jumping and changing direction.

Area/equipment
Indoor or outdoor area – Fast Foot Ladder or cones placed at 0.5 metre intervals.

Description
The player performs double-footed single jumps, i.e. 1 jump between each rung or cone. On reaching the end of the ladder, the player turns around and jumps back.

Key teaching points
- Maintain correct jumping form/mechanics
- The emphasis is on the speed of the jumps *not* the height
- Start slowly and increase the speed but do not lose control, i.e. avoid feeling as though you are going to 'fall over the edge of a cliff' when you reach the end of the drill

Sets and reps
2 sets of 2 reps with a 1-minute recovery between each set.

Variations/progressions
- Backward jumps down the ladder or cones
- Perform two jumps forwards and one jump back
- Sideways jumps down the ladder or cones
- Perform sideways jumps, 2 forwards and 1 back
- Perform hopscotch – 2 feet in one square and then 2 feet outside the square
- Perform left- and right-footed hops
- Increase the intensity – replace ladders/cones with 18–30 cm hurdles and perform the drills detailed above

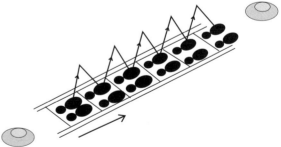

Key	
Feet together	
Jump	
Direction of Movement	

Figure 5.9 Plyometrics – Low-impact, quick jumps

DRILL   PLYOMETRIC CIRCUIT

Aim
To develop explosive multi-directional speed, agility and quickness.

Area/equipment
Indoor or outdoor area – place ladders, hurdles (which can be substituted with tackle shields or bags on the ground) and cones in a circuit formation (*see* fig. 5.10).

Description
The players jump, hop and zig-zag their way through the circuit as stipulated by the coach.

Key teaching points
- Maintain the correct mechanics for each part of the circuit
- Ensure that there is a smooth transfer from running to jumping movements and vice-versa

Sets and reps
5 circuits with a 1-minute recovery between each circuit.

Variations/progressions
- Work in pairs. 1 player completes the circuit while their partner feeds the ball at various points around the circuit for the player to pass back, dive on, etc.
- Introduce tackle bag/shield hits into the circuit

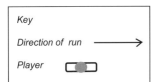

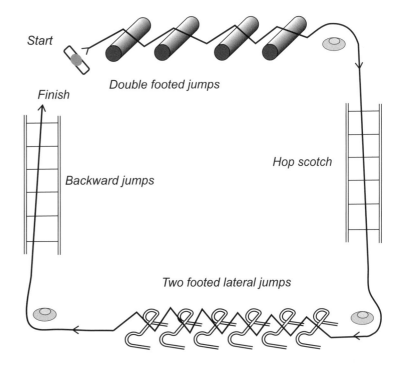

Figure 5.10 Plyometric circuit

DRILL PLYOMETRICS – DROP-JUMPS

Aim
To develop explosive multi-directional speed.

Area/equipment
Indoor or outdoor area with a cushioned or grassy landing surface. A stable platform or bench to jump from of variable height (40–90 cm) depending on the stage in the season.

Description
The player stands on the platform and jumps off with their feet together, lands on the balls of the feet and then accelerates away for 5 metres.

Key teaching points
- Do not land flat-footed
- Do not sink into the hips on landing
- Maintain a strong core
- Keep the head up – this will help to align the spine

Sets and reps
2 sets of 10 reps with a 3-minute recovery between each set.

Variations/progressions
- Perform backward drop-jumps, turning through 180° before sprinting off
- Perform side drop-jumps, turning and sprinting off
- Perform drop-jumps with a mid-air twist so that the player faces the platform
- Include a ball for the players to accelerate on to

CHAPTER 6 — EXPRESSION OF POTENTIAL

TEAM GAMES IN PREPARATION FOR THE NEXT LEVEL

This stage is quite short in duration, but very important, bringing together all the elements of the continuum into a highly competitive situation involving other players. Short, high-intensity 'tag' type games and random agility tests work really well here. The key is to fire up your players – for them to perform fast, explosive and controlled movements that leave them exhilarated – mentally and physically ready for the next stage of training or the game on Saturday.

DRILL 'BRITISH BULLDOG'

Aim
To practise multi-directional, explosive movements in a pressure situation.

Area/equipment
Outdoor or indoor area of approximately 20 square metres and around 20 cones to mark out starting and finishing lines.

Description
One player is nominated and situated in the centre of the grid; the rest stand at one side of the square. On the coach's call all the players attempt to get to the opposite side of the square without being caught by the player in the middle. When the player in the middle captures another player, they then join the player in the middle and help to capture more 'prisoners'.

Key teaching points
- Ensure that correct mechanics are used at all times
- Ensure that all players keep their head and eyes up to avoid collisions with others

Sets and reps
Play 'British Bulldog' for approximately 3–4 minutes before moving on to the more technical aspects of the game.

Variations/progressions
The player in the middle attempts to touch other players with the ball using either a pass or a grubber kick in order to capture them.

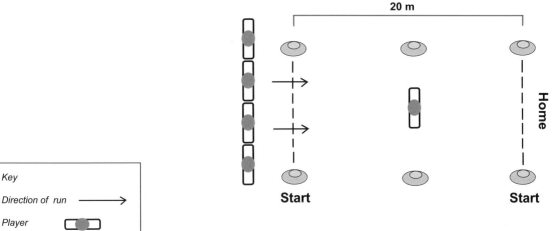

Figure 6.1 British Bulldog

DRILL CIRCLE BALL

Aim
To practise using explosive evasive skills.

Area/equipment
Outdoor or indoor area. Players make a circle approximately 15 metres in diameter (depending on the size of the squad).

Description
One or two players stand in the centre of the circle while the players on the outside have 1 or 2 balls. The object is for the players on the outside to try and make contact (by throwing the balls) with the players on the inside. The players on the inside try to avoid or dodge the ball. The winners are the pair who have the least number of hits during their 'centre phase'.

Key teaching points
■ Ensure that the central players use the correct mechanics

Sets and reps
Each pair to stay in the centre area for 45 seconds

Variations/progressions
■ Ball to be grubber-kicked
■ Players in the middle have to hold on to each other

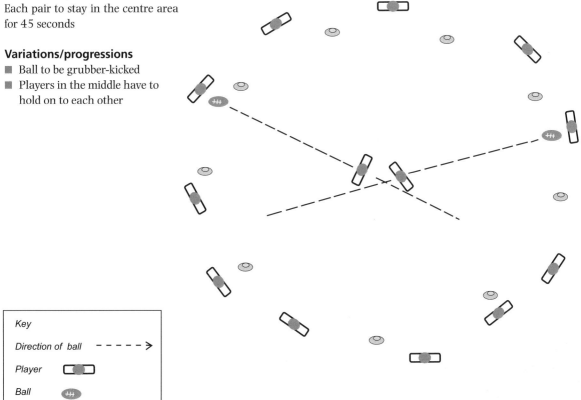

Key

Direction of ball – – – – →

Player

Ball

Figure 6.2 Circle ball

DRILL   'ROBBING THE NEST'

Aim
To practise multi-directional, explosive speed, agility and quickness.

Area/equipment
Outdoor or indoor area – cones and balls. Mark out a 20 metre square with a centre circle measuring approximately 2 metres in diameter. Place a number of balls in the centre circle.

Description
Two nominated players protect the nest of balls, with the rest of the players standing on the outside of the square area. The game starts when the outside players all run in and try to steal the balls from the nest by dribbling to the outside/safe zone of the square. The two defenders of the nest try to prevent the robbers from getting the balls to the safe zone by stopping them with fair tackles. For every successful tackle, the ball is returned to the centre circle.

Key teaching points
- Ensure that correct mechanics are used at all times
- Encourage players to dodge, swerve, weave, side-step, etc.

Sets and reps
Each pair defends for approximately 45 seconds.

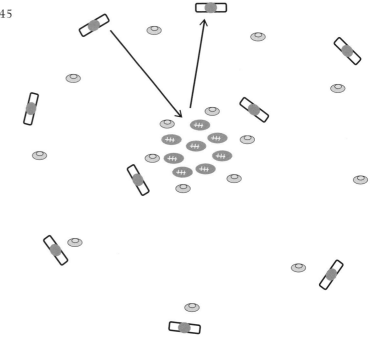

Key

Direction of running ⟶

Player

Ball

Figure 6.3 Robbing the nest

DRILL ODD ONE OUT

Aim
To practise speed, agility and quickness in a competitive environment.

Area/equipment
Outdoor or indoor area – cones and balls. Mark out a circle of 20–25 metres in diameter and a centre circle of approximately 2 metres in diameter. Place a number of balls in the centre area; you should have one fewer balls than the number of players present.

Description
The players are situated on the outside of the larger circle. On the coach's first call, the players start running around the larger circle. On the coach's second call they go and get a ball from the centre circle as quickly as possible. The player who misses out is the 'odd man out' and performs a rugby skill drill as directed by the coach. He retires from the game, the coach then removes another ball and the process is repeated.

Key teaching points
- Ensure that correct mechanics are used at all times
- Remind the players to be aware of the other players around them

Sets and reps
Play the game until a winner emerges

Variations/progressions
Work in pairs – i.e. one ball between two players.

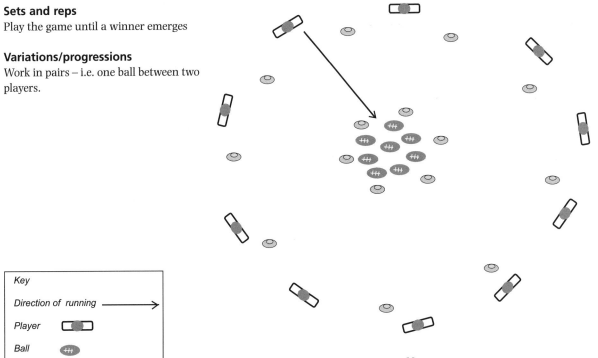

Key

Direction of running ——————→

Player

Ball

Figure 6.4 Odd one out

DRILL CONE TURNS

Aim
To practise multi-directional speed, agility and quickness.

Area/equipment
Outdoor or indoor area – 50 small cone markers. Mark out the area approximately 20 metres square and place the cones in and around the grid – 25 of the cones should be turned upside-down.

Description
Working in two small teams (2–3 players), one team attempts to turn over the upright cones and the other team to turn over the upside-down cones. The winner is the team that has the largest number of cones its way up after 60 seconds.

Key teaching points
- Ensure that players initiate good arm-drive after turning a cone
- Encourage players to use correct multi-directional mechanics
- Be aware of other players around the area

Sets and reps
A game should last for about 60 seconds.

Variations/progressions
Use 4 teams and allocate 4 different-coloured cones.

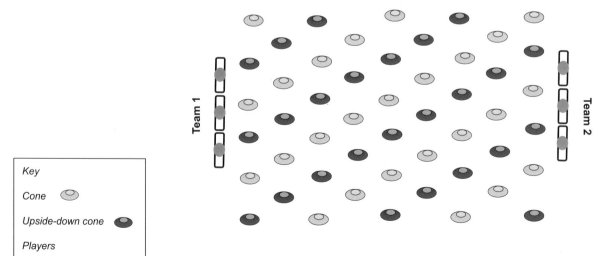

Key	
Cone	⬭
Upside-down cone	⬬
Players	

Figure 6.5 Cone turns

CHAPTER 7 POSITION-SPECIFIC DRILLS

In this section examples are provided of position-specific patterns of movement. By combining all areas of the SAQ Continuum – including techniques, equipment and drills – into game – and position-specific situations, you can improve and perfect the movement skills required by the players to succeed.

The primary aim is to improve the explosive speed, precision, control, power and co-ordination necessary for specific movements required by positions in all areas of the field. These are best introduced when the foundation work of SAQ has been mastered and during training sessions which are used to focus on the positional techniques of individual players.

DRILL VISUAL ACUITY DEVELOPMENT

Aim

To develop fast, accurate catching skills. To develop the players' visual skills in following the ball in flight.

Area/equipment

Outdoor or indoor area – Visual Acuity Ring (or a plastic hoop with coloured tape attached at 4 equal intervals in 4 different colours).

Description

Working in pairs approximately 5 metres apart, the ring is tossed so that it rotates through the air and is caught by the player on a colour nominated by the coach.

Key teaching points

- Keep the head still – move the eyes to track the ring
- Work off the balls of the feet at all times
- The hands should be out and in front of the body 'ready' to catch the ring

Sets and reps

2 set of 20 reps with a 1-minute recovery between each set.

Variations/progressions

Turn and catch.

DRILL

PERIPHERAL AWARENESS

Aim
To develop peripheral awareness – this will help the players move quickly to detect and react to the ball coming at them from all angles.

Area/equipment
Outdoor or indoor area – Peripheral Vision Stick or a stick or cane with coloured tape on the end. A corner flag could also be used.

Description
Working in pairs with player 2 behind the active player 1 who stands in a ready position. Player 2 holds the stick and moves it from behind player 1 into their field of vision. As soon as player 1 detects the stick they clap both hands over the ball at the end of the stick.

Key teaching points
- Player 1 should work off the balls of the feet and in a slightly crouched position with the hands out 'ready'
- Player 2 must be careful not to touch any part of player 1's body with the stick
- Player 2 should vary the speed at which the stick is brought into player 1's field of vision

Sets and reps
2 sets of 20 reps with no recovery between each rep and a 1-minute recovery between each set.

Variations/progressions
Instead of using a Peripheral Vision Stick, throw balls from behind player 1 that they have to fend off.

DRILL

BUNT BAT

Aim
To develop lightning quick hand–eye co-ordination.

Area/equipment
Outdoor or indoor area. A Bunt Bat (or a stick with 3 different coloured tapes positioned equally along the length), tennis balls or bean bags.

Description
Working in pairs, one of the players holds the Bunt Bat. His partner stands approximately 3–4 metres away and throws a ball or bean bag, simultaneously calling the colour of the ball on the Bunt Bat. The player's task is to fend off the ball or bean bag with the appropriate coloured ball on the Bunt Bat.

Key teaching points
- Start throwing the balls or bean bags slowly and gradually build up the speed
- Player should be in a 'set' position

Sets and reps
3 sets of 25 reps with a 30-second recovery between each set.

Variations/progressions
- Use different-coloured balls or bean bags. When the ball or bean bag has been thrown, it is to be fended off with the correspondingly coloured ball on the Bunt Bat
- The player stands on an agility disc while performing the drill

POSITION – DEFENCE
DRILL **DRIFT DEFENCE**

Aim
To develop explosive, co-ordinated linear and lateral movements used in drift defence.

Area/equipment
Indoor or outdoor grid, 15 square metres, split into a 10- and 5-metre area. Cones, 5 tackle shields or body armour sets and 4 Side-Steppers.

Description
Working with 9 players, split them into a defensive group of 4 (group D) and an attacking group of 5 (group A) (*see* fig. 7.1). Group D wears the Side-Steppers and lines up on the outside of the grid at the 10-metre line marked out by the cones. Group A wears the body armour or holds the shields and stands on the opposite side of the grid with the 5-metre line in front of them. Group A forms a line of 4 players with the extra player 2 metres behind. On the coach's call the attacking group starts moving forwards towards the 5-metre line, the extra player moving laterally behind them and then accelerating through one of the gaps. The defenders start moving towards the attackers. As soon as the extra player crosses the line, the defenders block the attack. One of the outside attacking players will be left free while the defenders concentrate on the extra player and the support players to either side.

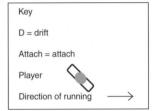

Key

D = drift

Attach = attach

Player

Direction of running

Key teaching points
- Maintain correct running form/mechanics when moving linearly and laterally
- Player 1 should use short, explosive steps and a strong arm-drive, particularly during the acceleration phase
- Encourage both the attacking and defending players to communicate

Sets and reps
2 sets of 6 reps plus a contrast run and a 3-minute recovery between each set.

Variations/progressions
Introduce a ball.

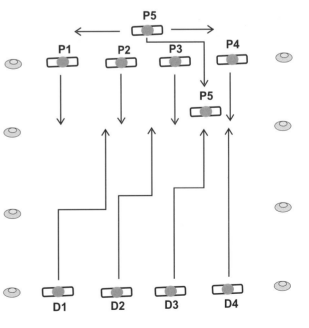

Figure 7.1 Resisted drift defence

POSITION – DEFENCE
DRILL EXPLOSIVE TACKLING

Aim
To develop explosive tackling designed to knock and drive the ball-carrier backwards.

Area/equipment
Indoor or outdoor large area – shield, Side-Stepper and 3 cones placed in a straight line approximately 5 metres apart.

Description
Player 1 wears the Side-Stepper and stands at cone A, Player 2 stands at cone C holding a tackle shield. On the coach's signal player 2 starts walking towards the centre cone B, while player 1 accelerates towards cone B. Player 1 then executes a tackle on player 2, driving him backwards to cone C.

Key teaching points
- Maintain correct running form/mechanics
- Ensure that players use short fast steps
- Work off the balls of the feet
- Keep the spine straight
- Ensure that players use the correct techniques when tackling
- Ensure that players remove the Side-Steppers to perform the contrast run

Sets and reps
3 sets of 6 reps plus 1 contrast run with a 3-minute recovery between each set.

Variations/progressions
- Player 2 (with a shield) moves sideways
- Introduce an extra player with a shield; player 1 then completes a tackle on each player

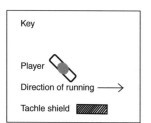

Key

Player

Direction of running ———→

Tackle shield ▨▨▨▨

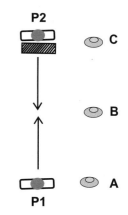

Figure 7.2 Attacking the opposition's position

POSITION – DEFENCE

DRILL AGILITY RUN – ZIG-ZAG DRIFT DEFENCE

Aim
To develop a co-ordinated, explosive defensive line. To cut down the space quickly in a controlled manner.

Area/equipment
Indoor or outdoor large area. Mark out a grid using 10–12 cones in 2 lines of 5–6. Stagger the cones so that the line makes a zig-zag formation (*see* fig. 7.3a). On one side locate 5 or 6 shields for contact.

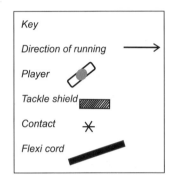

Description
6 players stand in single file just outside the grid. The first player enters the grid sideways and facing the shield. The drill starts as the first player tackles the shield then angles backwards to the second cone. The second player now commences the drill in the same way. Each of the remaining players now enters the grid so that all are in the grid working as a co-ordinated drift defence. When the first player completes their final hit, they accelerate back around to the first cone to start again.

Key teaching points
- Players to work in a co-ordinated manner
- Work off the balls of the feet
- Use strong arm mechanics
- Use short steps
- Keep head up and spine straight
- Ensure contact phase is technically correct

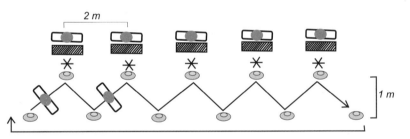

Figure 7.3(a) Zig-zag drift defence agility run

Sets and reps
3 sets with a 2-minute recovery between each set. A set is 2 lengths of the grid. (The recovery time should be increased to 3 minutes when the players are performing the drill while resisted.)

Variations/progressions
- Introduce resistance by using Viper Belts (*see* fig. 7.3b)
- Vary the tackle made (**NB:** ensure that the players perform a one-rep contrast)

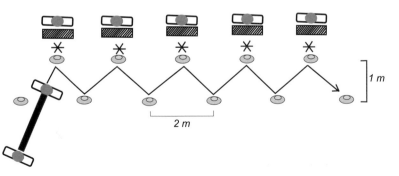

Figure 7.3(b) Zig-zag drift defence agility run with resistance

DRILL LATERAL EXPLOSIVE TACKLING

Aim

To develop quick, explosive lateral movement while tackling from a side-on position.

Area/equipment

Indoor or outdoor large area. Mark out a grid using 3 cones, placing them in a straight line (as shown in fig 7.4). Tackle bags and a Viper Belt with a Flexi-cord attached.

Description

Player 1 wears the Viper Belt and stands side-on to the centre cone B. Player 2 stands on cone C holding the Flexi-cord so that it is taut. On the coach's signal player 1 moves sideways and tackles the bag which is being held by the coach.

Key teaching points

- Do not cross the feet during the lateral movement
- Work off the balls of the feet
- Do not sink into the hips
- Ensure that when executing the tackle the head is kept up and behind the player being tackled
- Thrust hips upwards on impact during the tackling phase

Sets and reps

1 set of 8 tackles, 4 to the left and 4 to the right, with a contrast tackle on each side and a 3-minute recovery before the next drill.

Variations/progressions

Replace the tackle bag with a player carrying a ball in their hands (they should wear body armour for protection). The tackled player attempts to place the ball for the support player.

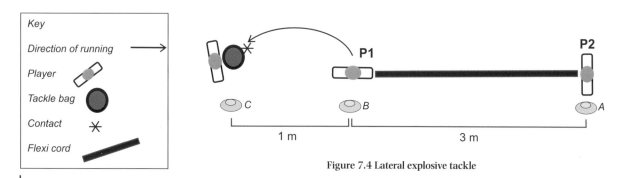

Figure 7.4 Lateral explosive tackle

DRILL | *POSITION – DEFENCE*
OFFSIDE TO ONSIDE ASSISTED/RESISTED DRIVE

Aim
To develop explosive backward running and an explosive transfer into a forward drive. **NB** This drill will also help prevent players hitting a ruck or a maul from a side-on position, which is in an illegal move.

Area/equipment
Indoor or outdoor area – 1 Viper Belt, 2 tackle shields and 7 cones set up as shown in fig. 7.5.

Description
Players 1 and 2 are connected by the Viper Belt, player 1 starts at cone A and player 2 at cone C (the flexi-cord will be taut). Players 3 and 4 each hold a tackle shield and stand in the centre of the grid, approximately 2 metres from the drive cones D and E. On the coach's call, player 1 explodes backwards (assisted) to the drive cones D and E before exploding forwards (resisted) to drive players 3 and 4 backwards. Player 1 then returns to start position B and repeats the drill.

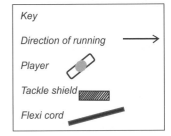

Key teaching points
- Maintain correct running form/mechanics, particularly when moving backwards
- Use short, explosive arm movements
- Use short, explosive steps during the transfer phase from backward to forward running
- Ensure player 1 keeps his head up and his spine straight when dropping his body height to drive players 3 and 4 backwards.
- Player 2 must remain stationary at all times

Sets and reps
2 sets of 8 reps plus 1 contrast run per set, with a walk-back recovery between each rep and a 3-minute recovery between sets.

Variations/progressions
- Introduce the ball just in front of cones D and E for the player to pick up and drive
- Coach to pass the ball to player 1 just prior to the drive phase

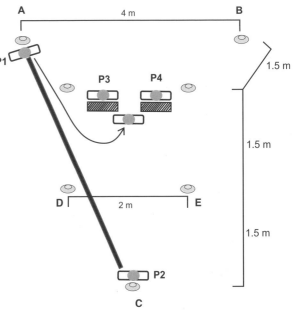

Figure 7.5 Assisted and resisted drive

POSITION – DEFENCE

DRILL ALIGNMENT AND COMMUNICATION

Aim
To develop positional awareness, speed, co-ordination and communication between players for drift defence.

Area/equipment
Large indoor or outdoor area – 2 Break-Away Belts and 12 cones (3 x 4 different colours). Mark out an area of 10 square metres with 3 cones of the same colour on each side of the square, with a distance of 1 m between them (*see* fig. 7.6)

Description
Three players are joined together with 2 Break-Away Belts, i.e. the player in the middle is attached to a player on both his left and his right. On the coach's call all 3 players move to a set of coloured cones and touch one cone each without breaking the belts. The coach immediately calls another set of cones either behind or to the side of the players, who move to touch these cones, again without breaking the belts.

Key teaching points
- Maintain correct running form/mechanics
- Use a strong arm-drive, particularly when changing direction
- Do not cross the feet or skip when changing direction
- Encourage good communication between players

Sets and reps
3 sets of 8 reps (calls from coach) with a 2-minute rest between sets.

Variations/progressions
Set up a hexagon grid using 18 cones (3 x 6 different colours).

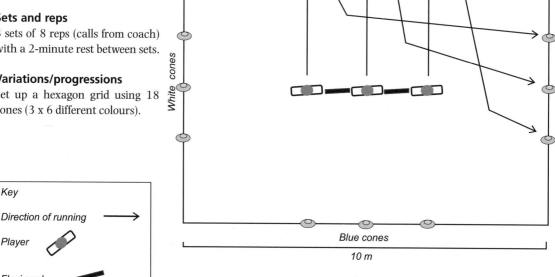

Figure 7.6 Alignment and communication drift defence

POSITION – DEFENCE
DRILL　DRIFT DEFENCE WITH BREAK-AWAY BELTS

Aim
To develop balance, co-ordination and positional awareness.

Area/equipment
Large indoor or outdoor area – 2 Break-Away Belts for every 3 players, and 12 cones. Mark out a zig-zag channel of approximately 10 metres in width and 25 metres in length (*see* fig. 7.7).

Description
Players work in groups of 3 and are joined together by the Break-Away Belts – i.e. the player in the middle will be wearing both belts, 1 attached to the player on their right and 1 attached to the player on their left. Players work down the zig-zag channel, moving from side to side and trying to maintain a constant distance between them. If a gap becomes too big the belt will break, which means that in a game the defensive line could be breached by an opposing team. On reaching the penultimate set of cones the 3 players run backwards to the next set of cones before continuing forwards to the end of the channel.

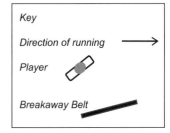

Key teaching points
- Maintain correct running form/mechanics
- Use short, explosive arm movements
- Ensure players use short steps when moving laterally
- Do not cross feet or skip
- Increase arm speed when changing direction
- Keep the head up and look forwards
- Encourage use of peripheral vision to allow players to monitor their team-mates' positions

Sets and reps
2 sets of 5 reps plus 1 rep without the belts on, with a walk-back recovery between each rep and a 2-minute recovery between sets.

Variations/progressions
Increase the size of the grid and introduce a fourth or fifth player.

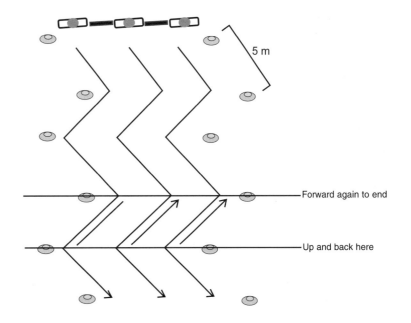

Figure 7.7 Drift defence with Break-Away Belts

POSITION – DEFENCE – BACK ROW

DRILL RESISTED BACK SCRUM DOUBLE TACKLE

Aim

To develop explosive speed and power from the back of the scrum, and initiate a first hit or tackle and then a second tackle on the opposing support player.

Area/equipment

Indoor or outdoor area – 1 Viper Belt, 2 tackle shields/suits and 6 cones set up as shown (*see* fig. 7.8).

Description

Player 1 and player 2 are connected by the Viper Belt. Player 1 starts in a kneeling position between the cones marked A. On the coach's call, player 1 drives forwards and initiates a tackle on player 3. As this tackle is initiated, player 4 moves from his start position directly behind player 3 to his left or right side. Player 1 disengages from the first tackle and initiates a second tackle on player 4.

Key teaching points

- Maintain correct running form/mechanics
- Player 1 to use an explosive arm- and leg-drive to get up as quickly as possible from his starting position
- When dropping the body height for the tackles, ensure that player 1 keeps his head up and his spine straight
- Player 2 remains stationary at all times

Sets and reps

2 sets of 6 reps plus 1 contrast run, with a walk-back recovery between each rep and a 3-minute recovery between sets.

Variations/progressions

2 rugby balls can be introduced and placed one either side of player 3 on cones B. Player 4 steps over the ball as they move forwards and player 1's second tackle is then to drive player 4 off the ball.

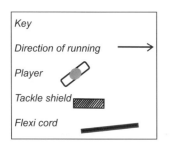

Key

Direction of running →

Player

Tackle shield

Flexi cord

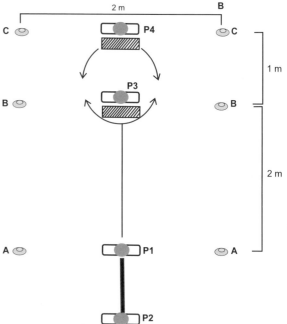

Figure 7.8 Back row – resisted double tackle from the back of the scrum

POSITION – DEFENCE – 'TIGHT 5'

DRILL *LOW EXPLOSIVE DRIVING*

Aim
To develop controlled explosive movement while in a low driving position, particularly useful for props, hookers and second rows who work in close contact with the opposition on a regular basis throughout the game.

Area/equipment
Indoor or outdoor area – 1 Viper Belt, a set of goalposts, 2 metal/wooden stakes and 20–25 m of thin cord. Place the stakes 4 m out from each goalpost, tie the cord around the 2 stakes and the posts and then across the middle so that the cord is approximately 4 feet off the floor. Place 5 cones in a 'W' formation (*see* fig. 7.9a)

Description
Player 1 and player 2 are connected by the Viper Belt. Player 1 starts on one side of the goalpost and accelerates towards cone 1, runs backwards at an angle to cone 2, forwards to cone 3, etc. finishing at the side of the far goalpost. Player 2 works up, back and across with player 1 maintaining a constant resistance.

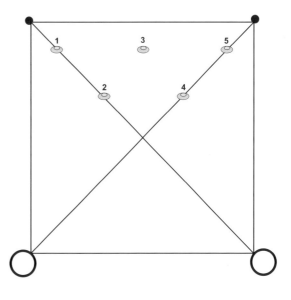

Figure 7.9(a) Low explosive driving – drill area

Key teaching points
■ Ensure that player 1 keeps his head up
■ Use a strong arm-drive
■ Use short, precise steps, particularly when going backwards

Sets and reps
1 set of 6 reps plus 2 contrast runs, 1 to the left and 1 to the right with a 30-second recovery between each rep.

Variations/progressions
■ Perform the drill backwards or laterally
■ Perform the drill while running with the ball

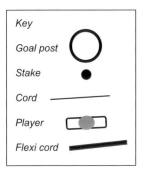

Key
Goal post ◯
Stake ●
Cord ——
Player ▭
Flexi cord ▬

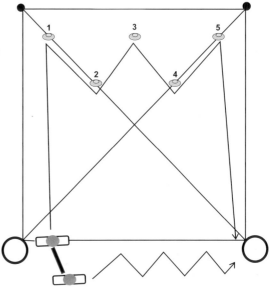

Figure 7.9(b) Low explosive driving drill

DRILL *FRONT-ROW EXPLOSIVE SCRUM*

Aim
To develop controlled explosive and balanced engagement at the front row of the scrum.

Area/equipment
Outdoor area – 3 Viper Belts and a scrum machine.

Description
All 3 members of the front row wear a Viper Belt with 3 other players providing resistance from behind. The flexi-cords should be stretched to approximately double their resting length. The front row bind, squat and then drive into the scrum machine, hitting the machine back by 0.5 m. They disengage, set and repeat the drill with the 3 players behind taking a short step forwards to keep the resistance constant.

Key teaching points
- The front row should use very short steps
- The front row should use correct scrummaging technique
- Ensure that the players' heads are up and their spines in a straight line

Sets and reps
2 sets of 10 reps plus 2 contrast hits per set, with a walk-back recovery between each rep and a 3-minute recovery between sets.

Variations/progressions
5-second constant drive of the scrummaging machine (2 sets of 5 reps with 1 contrast)

POSITION – FORWARDS

DRILL · ATTACKING THE OPPOSITION'S POSSESSION

Aim

To develop explosive speed and agility in the defensive forwards during close-contact work, where a ball has been moved from the initial breakdown spot to a new point of attack.

Area/equipment

Indoor or outdoor area – 1 Viper Belt, 2 tackle shields/suits and 10 cones set up as shown.

Description

Players 1 and 2 are connected by the Viper Belt and player 1 lies down between the start cones A. On the coach's call, player 1 explodes up and out towards a nominated cone (1–4) which he touches (these cones represent the initial breakdown spot). Player 1 then explodes to the left (cone B) or the right (cone C) as nominated by the coach, where he initiates a tackle on player 3 or 4. After the initial touch, player 2 can move across with player 1 but resistance must be maintained.

Key teaching points

- Maintain correct running form/mechanics
- Ensure that the player keeps his head up and his spine straight when dropping the body height for tackles
- Use an explosive arm- and leg-drive on the initial get-up
- Ensure that the player uses short steps when changing direction
- Do not cross feet

Sets and reps

1 set of 6 reps plus 1 contrast run, with a walk-back recovery between each rep.

Variations/progressions

On cones B and C, replace the tackle shields with tackle bags. Lay these down with a ball on one side, so that player 1 picks up the ball and steps over the bag before going to the ground and laying the ball back for a support player to pick up and drive on – *see* fig. 7.10b.

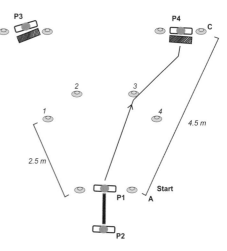

Figure 7.10(a) Attacking the opposition's possession and getting to the second breakdown (i)

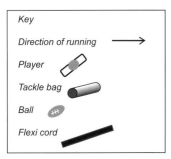

Key	
Direction of running	⟶
Player	
Tackle bag	
Ball	
Flexi cord	

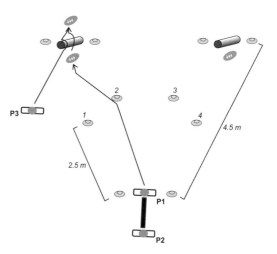

Figure 7.10(b) Attacking the opposition's possession and getting to the second breakdown (ii)

DRILL   RESISTED LINE-OUT

Aim
To develop explosive vertical power and explosive movement, balance and control for the support lifters.

Area/equipment
Indoor or outdoor area – if possible, conduct the drill in the relevant position on the pitch. 2 Viper Belts, a 3–5 kg Jelly Ball and 5 cones set up as shown.

Description
Players 2 and 4 and 3 and 5 are connected together respectively by Viper Belts. Player 1 stands in the middle between cones 3 and 4. Players 2 and 3 – the 'lifters' – stand 'ready' on cones 3 and 4. Players 4 and 5 stand on cones 2 and 5 respectively while player 6, the hooker, prepares to throw the ball in. On the coach's call, players 2 and 3 move in and back then in again towards player 1; they then lift player 1 into the air. Player 1, the jumper, holding the Jelly Ball brings his hands up above his head as he jumps/lifts. Player 1 then drops the Jelly Ball to one side and receives the rugby ball thrown in by player 6. Player 6 runs a support loop to receive the ball from player 1.

Key teaching points
- Player 1 must use good jump mechanics
- Players 2 and 3 (the jumpers) to use short explosive arm-drives and steps
- Player 6 must use an explosive arm-drive to accelerate on the support run
- Players 4 and 5 to remain stationary

Sets and reps
1 set of 5 reps plus 1 contrast drill, with a walk-back recovery between each rep and a 3-minute recovery before the next drill.

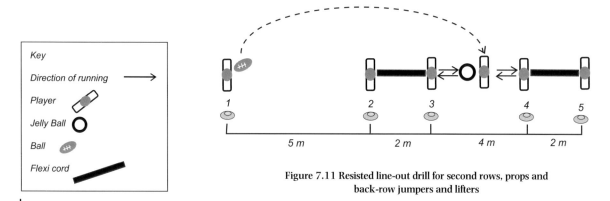

Key

Direction of running ⟶

Player

Jelly Ball O

Ball

Flexi cord

1   2   3   4   5

5 m   2 m   4 m   2 m

Figure 7.11 Resisted line-out drill for second rows, props and back-row jumpers and lifters

DRILL *FORWARD EXPLOSION INTO THE LINE-OUT*

Aim
To develop explosive and controlled movement into forward space in the line-out.

Area/equipment
Indoor or outdoor area – if possible conduct the drill in the relevant position on the pitch. 1 Viper Belt and 3 cones set up as shown.

Description
Player 1 and player 2 are connected by the Viper Belt. Player 3 stands on cone 3 which is place 2 metres from the 5-metre line. On a signal by the hooker (player 4), player 3 moves back and into the line-out. Player 1 explodes forwards into the space between cones 2 and 3 and jumps to receive the ball thrown in by player 4, the hooker. Player 2 works with player 1 maintaining a constant resistance. During the jump phase of the drill, player 2 kneels down to provide extra resistance for the vertical take-off.

Key teaching points
■ Use short, explosive steps and arm-drives when moving forwards
■ Use good jump mechanics and a double arm-drive on the vertical take-off
■ Player 3 must turn into the line in an explosive blocking movement

Sets and reps
1 set of 8 reps plus 1 contrast drill with a walk-back recovery between each rep.

Variations/progressions
Have 2 line-out teams working against each other, 1 attacking and 1 defending.

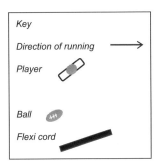

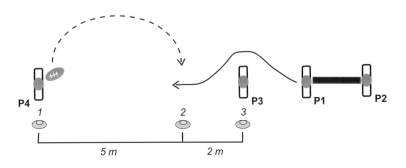

Figure 7.12 Second row and number 8 forward explosion into the line-out

DRILL *CENTRES' MIDFIELD PENETRATION*

Aim

To develop controlled, explosive acceleration and change-of-direction ability for midfield penetration.

Area/equipment

Indoor or outdoor large area – 3 ladders, 5 cones and rugby balls. Place a ladder out in an inverted 'L' position and a second ladder in the same position 2 metres away from the first. Place the third ladder between the other two in a straight line, a cone 1 metre away from the start of each ladder and a cone 1 metre away from the end of the two 'L' shaped ladders.

Description

3 players work through the ladders simultaneously performing fast feet drills. Players 1 and 2 transfer to lateral drills as the ladder dictates, while player 3 continues with the linear run. Player 1 accelerates on to the ball fed in by the coach and passes the ball on to player 2. On receiving the ball player 2 cuts inside; player 1 also cuts inside. Player 3 now accelerates down the middle of the grid; player 2 dummies a pass to player 1 before offloading the ball to player 3 who explodes through the middle. Player 1 then straightens up his run to provide support to player 3, who passes the ball outside to player 1. Rotate the players' starting positions.

Key teaching points

- Maintain correct running form/mechanics
- Re-assert powerful arm mechanics after passing the ball
- Use the correct technical skills when receiving and passing the ball
- Use clear visual and verbal communication

Sets and reps

3 sets of 6 reps with a 1-minute recovery between each set. Players should perform 2 reps as player 1, 2 as player 2 and 2 as player 3.

Variations/progressions

- Introduce 2 players who defend the central area
- Vary the types of pass used, and vary the player taking the ball

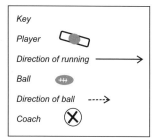

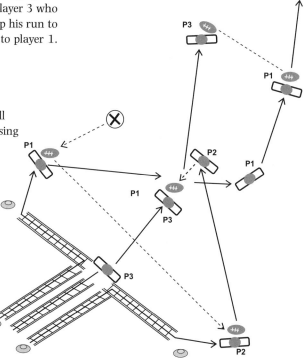

Figure 7.13 Centres' midfield penetration, fast feet, acceleration, switch and a dummy pass

POSITION – CENTRES

| DRILL | SIDE-STEP AND LINEAR ACCELERATION |

Aim

To develop explosive side-steps just in front of the defensive press, to cause uncertainty in the defensive alignment and create a gap to penetrate.

Area/equipment

Indoor or outdoor large area – Viper Belt with 2 flexi-cords attached, 1 to each side. Place 6 cones in 2 zig-zag lines of 3 with a 1-metre gap between the 2 lines (*see* fig. 7.14a).

Description

Working in groups of 3, player 1 wears the Viper Belt while players 2 and 3 hold a Flexi-cord each – one to the left of player 1 and one to the right. The drill commences with player 1 side-stepping to the cones. At the last cone he accelerates forwards. Players 2 and 3 immediately move directly behind him to provide resistance from the rear.

Key teaching points

- Player 1 must use the correct running form/mechanics
- Player 1 must use short, explosive steps and a strong arm-drive
- Player 1 must push off the outside foot when changing direction and not pull with the lead foot
- Player 1 must stay tall and work off the balls of the feet
- Players 3 and 4 must concentrate and keep resistance constant for player 1

Sets and reps

2 sets of 5 reps plus a contrast run, with a walk-back recovery between each rep and a 3-minute recovery between each set.

Variations/progressions

- Once the players have mastered the basic drill, player 1 can perform the drill with the ball in their hands
- Introduce a fourth player who runs at an angle to receive a pass from player 1 during the linear explosive phase (*see* fig. 7.14c)
- Introduce a tackle shield to the linear explosive phase

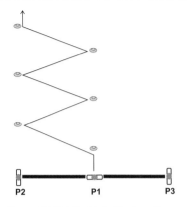
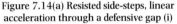

Figure 7.14(a) Resisted side-steps, linear acceleration through a defensive gap (i)

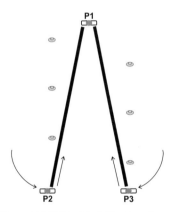

Figure 7.14(b) Resisted side-steps, linear acceleration through a defensive gap (ii)

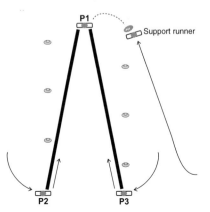

Figure 7.14(c) Resisted side-steps, linear acceleration through a defensive gap with support runner

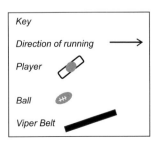

Key

Direction of running →

Player

Ball

Viper Belt

DRILL HIT-AND-DRIVE BACKWARDS – TACKLE

Aim
To develop an explosive front-on tackle that not only stops the defender but drives and knocks him backwards.

Area/equipment
Indoor or outdoor area – 1 Viper Belt with 2 Flexi-cords attached, a tackle bag and 4 cones set up as shown.

Description
Players should work in groups of 4, with players 1 and 2 connected by the Viper Belt and the 2 Flexi-cords. Player 1 starts in a head-first prone position between the cones marked A. Players 3 and 4 hold a tackle bag sideways on in front of player 1 (approximately 1 m away). Player 1 accelerates off the ground and thrusts upwards with the body and the arms to drive the tackle bag up and backwards.

Key teaching points
- The transfer from ground to upwards and forwards thrust should be a smooth and continuous movement
- Player 2 remains stationary throughout the drill

Sets and reps
2 sets of 8 reps plus 2 contrast runs, with a walk-back recovery between each rep and a 3-minute recovery between each set.

Variations/progressions
The coach rolls a ball into the grid immediately after player 1 has made the tackle.

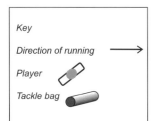

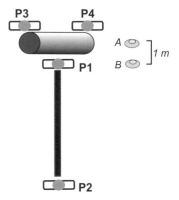

Figure 7.15 Explosive hit-and-drive backwards tackle

DRILL	*VISUAL ACUITY AND TRACKING*

Aim

To develop eye, hand and foot co-ordination, visual acuity and tracking between the scrum-half and the fly-half.

Area/equipment

Indoor or outdoor area – 5 rugby balls. Using an indelible marker, place the following symbols one on each panel at the end of each rugby ball.

Panel 1 = c , panel 2 = ? , panel 3 = w and panel 4 = v

On the opposite end of the ball, number the panels 1, 2, 3 and 4.

Description

The coach places the balls in a straight line 5 metres apart, ensuring that a number or shape is clearly visible on each one. The scrum-half stands in front of the first ball, accelerates towards it, scoops it up and passes it to the fly-half who is situated 10 metres to the left or right. As the ball is passed, the fly-half calls out which number or shape was showing on the ball as the scrum-half scooped it up.

Key teaching points

- Maintain correct running form/mechanics
- The scrum-half must 'show' the panel prior to passing it to the fly-half
- The fly-half must visually focus on the ball as it is scooped up and passed
- Use the correct passing and catching techniques

Sets and reps

2 sets of 4 reps (i.e. all 5 balls) with time between each rep to reset the balls and a 1-minute recovery between each set.

DRILL

EXPLOSIVE GROUND REACTION

Aim

To develop multi-directional explosive movements to gather and control the rugby ball rolled or thrown towards the scrum-half.

Area/equipment

Indoor or outdoor hard surfaced area – reaction ball.

Description

Players can work in pairs or against a wall. The reaction ball is thrown to land within 1 metre of the scrum-half, who attempts to catch it before the second bounce. Due to the shape of the ball it will bounce off the surface at different angles and different heights, forcing the scrum-half to react accordingly.

Key teaching points

- Bend at the knees and not at the waist
- Work off the balls of the feet
- Keep the hands 'ready' in front of the body
- Do not throw the ball hard – it will do the necessary work itself

Sets and reps

3 sets of 25 reps with a 1-minute recovery between each set.

Variations/progressions

Vary the starting position of the scrum-half, e.g. backwards, sideways, etc.

POSITION – SCRUM-HALF

DRILL — ASSISTED EXPLOSIVE RUNNING

Aim
To develop explosive acceleration and swerve-running from the back of the scrum, attacking the gap between the opposition's open side and fly-half.

Area/equipment
Indoor or outdoor area – 1 Viper Belt and 10 cones set up as shown. The 4 cones that are set up in a line 2 metres long represent the scrum-half's back row.

Description
Player 1 and player 2 are connected by the Viper Belt. The scrum-half (player 1) stands at the start cones while player 2 faces player 1 and starts to walk backwards to the cones marked B. Just before player 2 reaches the cones, player 1 accelerates to the left or right of the 4 cones marked A (back row) and swerves around cone C before straightening up their run.

Key teaching points
- Maintain correct running form/mechanics
- Work off the balls of the feet
- The scrum-half should use an explosive arm-drive and short, explosive steps
- Do not allow the feet to cross over
- Do not allow the player to sink into the hips
- Keep looking ahead

Sets and reps
2 sets of 10 reps plus 1 contrast run, with a walk-back recovery between each rep and a 3-minute recovery between each set.

Variations/progressions
Introduce a ball and a support runner (player 3). The scrum-half offloads the ball to the support runner after he has passed cone C and straightened up his run (*see* fig. 7.16b).

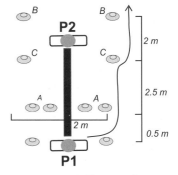

Figure 7.16(a) Scrum-half – assisted running

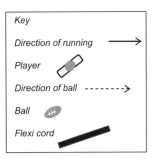

Key

Direction of running ⟶

Player

Direction of ball - - - - ->

Ball

Flexi cord

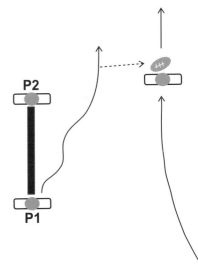

Figure 7.16(b) Scrum-half – assisted running with ball and support runner

DRILL   MULTI-DIRECTIONAL EXPLOSIVE MOVEMEN

Aim

To develop multi-directional, explosive movements to the ball and with the ball in hand for the scrum-half in the vulnerable positions at the base of the scrum and the side of a line-out.

Area/equipment

Indoor or outdoor area – rugby balls, 1 Viper Belt with 3 flexi-cords attached and 4 cones set up as shown.

Description

The scrum-half (player 1) wears the Viper Belt with flexi-cords attached from the back and both sides. Player 2 holds a slightly taut flexi-cord from behind and both players 3 and 4 form the sides of player 1. Player 1 stands between cones A (start line); the coach stands 3.5 m away between cones B with a number of rugby balls. The drill commences with the coach rolling a ball on the floor or tossing a ball in the air no more than 1 m away to the left, right or towards player 1. Player 1 either dives on or catches the ball and passes it to player 3 or 4.

Key teaching points

- The scrum-half should work off the balls of the feet so that he is ready to run
- Short steps must be used when moving laterally or on an angle
- The scrum-half should use an explosive arm-drive and short, explosive steps
- Players must not cross their feet or skip
- The scrum-half should stay tall for as long as possible and return to this position as quickly as possible after picking the ball up (this helps with acceleration)
- Players 2, 3 and 4 remain stationary
- Players 3 and 4 must be prepared to receive the ball from the scrum-half and return it promptly to the coach

Key

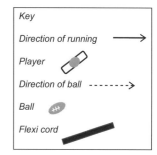

Direction of running	⟶
Player	⬭
Direction of ball	⇢
Ball	🏉
Flexi cord	▬

Sets and reps

2 sets of 8 reps plus 2 contrast runs per set with a walk-back recovery between each rep and a 3-minute recovery between each set.

Variations/progressions

Use a weighted rugby ball or a 3 kg Jelly Ball.

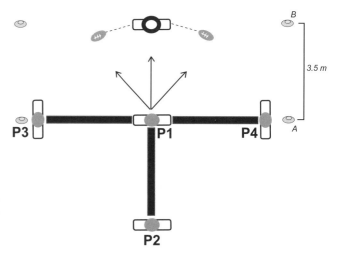

Figure 7.17 Scrum-half – base of scrum and side of line-out explosive movement

POSITION – FLY-HALF

DRILL ASSISTED AND RESISTED SUPPORT LOOP RUNS

Aim

To develop explosive support-loop running.

Area/equipment

Indoor or outdoor area – rugby balls, 1 Viper Belt and 4 cones set up as shown.

Description

Players should work in groups of 6 with players 1 and 2 connected by the Viper Belt. Players 3, 4, 5, and 6 stand in a line level with the cone marked B with approximately 5 metres between each player. Player 1, the fly-half, stands level with cone A, in front of and slightly to the left of player 3. Player 3 has the ball. The drill commences when player 1 accelerates into the gap between players 3 and 4 receiving a pass from player 3 and transferring it to player 4. The fly-half now loops around player 4 to receive the return pass. This is repeated until player 1 receives the final pass from player 6. Throughout the drill player 2 moves laterally across the grid and so provides a constant resistance for player 1.

Key teaching points

- Player 1 must work hard to maintain correct running form/mechanics during both the resisted and assisted phases
- Ensure that player 1, the fly-half, re-asserts a strong arm-drive when he has offloaded the ball
- Ensure that all players use the correct passing techniques

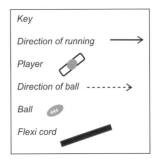

Key

Direction of running   ⟶

Player

Direction of ball   - - - - - ->

Ball

Flexi cord

Sets and reps

2 sets of 4 reps (2 to the left and 2 to the right) plus 2 contrast runs per set (1 to the left and 1 to the right), with a 30-second recovery between each rep and a 3-minute recovery between each set.

Variations/progressions

A very advanced progression – players 3, 4, 5 and 6 move forwards in a linear direction, which will require players 1 and 2 to move up and across while maintaining a constant resistance.

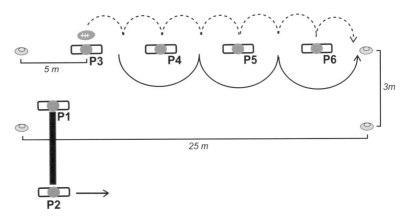

Figure 7.18 Assisted/resisted support loop runs

POSITION – WINGERS

| DRILL | **ACCELERATION – SWERVE – DECELERATION** |

Aim

To develop off-the-mark acceleration, explosive swerves and controlled deceleration before changing direction.

Area/equipment

Large indoor or outdoor area – 1 tackle bag, 2 ladders and 7 cones set up as shown.

Description

Player 1, the winger, accelerates down the first ladder then accelerates and swerve-runs between the cones for 15 m. On reaching the second ladder, the winger decelerates with control. The coach then nominates cone 1, 2 or 3, whereupon the winger changes direction and accelerates to that cone. At the cone he receives a pass, tackles a bag or receives a pass and chip-kicks.

Key teaching points

- Maintain correct running form/mechanics
- Lean back and fire the arms during the deceleration phase, but stay on the balls of the feet
- Stay tall and do not sink into the hips during the change of direction phase
- Do not cross feet or skip
- Ensure players use correct passing, tackling and kicking techniques as appropriate

Sets and reps

1 set of 6 reps with a walk-back recovery between each rep and a 3-minute recovery before the next drill.

Variations/progressions

On the first ladder vary the Fast Foot Ladder drills, e.g. 'icky shuffle', lateral, etc.

Key

Direction of running ——→

Player

Tackle bag

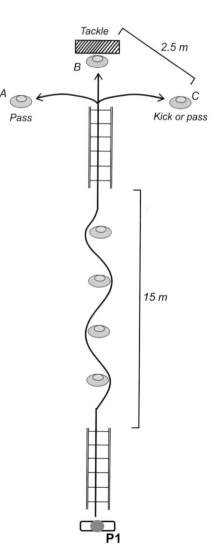

Figure 7.19 Wingers – acceleration – serve – deceleration

POSITION – WINGERS

| DRILL | ASSISTED/RESISTED TOW RUNS |

Aim

To develop explosive speed and control while swerve-running.

Area/equipment

Large indoor or outdoor area. For maximum benefit this drill should be performed in the relevant areas of the pitch, i.e. near the sideline. 2 Viper Belts, 2 flexi-cords and 5 cones in a straight line with a distance of 5 m between each cone.

Description

Players 1 and 2 are connected together by the Viper Belts and both flexi-cords. The drill commences with player 1 accelerating from the first cone around the second cone. Player 2 remains stationary – so that player 1 is resisted for the first 2 m – until player 1 has moved 2 m away. Due to the flexi-cords player 2 will then explode in pursuit of player 1. After the second cone, player 2 decelerates and player 1 accelerates again. This is repeated along the length of the grid.

Key teaching points

■ Maintain correct running form/mechanics
■ Use a strong arm-drive
■ Use short, explosive steps during the acceleration phase
■ Player 2 (the assisted player) must maintain an upright, forward lean and try not to resist by leaning back, as this will cause deceleration

Sets and reps

2 sets of 4 reps (each player completes 2 assisted and 2 resisted reps plus 1 contrast run each per set). Players should take a 20-second recovery between each rep and a 3-minute recovery between each set.

Variations/progressions

■ Players can run the grid with the ball in their hands
■ Introduce a tackle shield to the side of cones 2 and 4 for player 2 to shoulder out of the way

Key

Direction of running ⟶

Player ▱

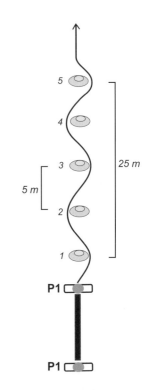

Figure 7.20 Wingers – assisted/resisted tow runs

POSITION – FULL-BACK AND WINGERS
COMING INTO THE LINE IN AN ARC

Aim

Modern rugby demands that wingers and full-backs time explosive angled and arced runs into the back line to penetrate the opposition's defensive line.

Area/equipment

Indoor or outdoor area. For maximum benefit this drill should be performed in the relevant areas of the pitch. An overspeed tow rope and cones set out to make arcs of approximately 40 m in length, starting on the outside and arcing in to the midfield areas.

Description

Players 1 and 2 are connected by the overspeed-tow-rope belts: player 1 is assisted from the front and player 2 resisted from the back. Player 3 holds the handle and provides different levels of overspeed. Player 1 will run the arc. Player 2 runs in a straight line away from player 3, who moves back towards the original starting-point of player 1. It is vital that player 3 continually watches player 1 to ensure that the correct level of assistance is being provided.

Key teaching points

- Players 1 and 2 should maintain correct running form/mechanics
- Player 1 must relax – do not resist the power
- Player 1 should lean slightly into the pull and not against it
- Player 2 should take short fast steps and avoid sinking into the hips
- Player 3 must keep an eye on player 1 – do not overload the power

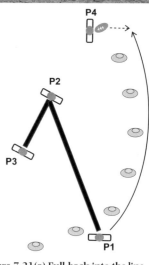

Figure 7.21(a) Full-back into the line – wingers receiving pass

Sets and reps

After 1 rep rotate the players as follows: the resisted player becomes assisted; the assisted player becomes player 3/control; and player 3/control becomes the resisted player. Each player is to perform 5 reps.

Variations/progressions

- Advanced – player 1 swerves in and out of some cones while running the arc
- At the end of the arc, when the full-back/winger is at maximum pace, an additional player (4) passes a ball to player 1 to control under pressure

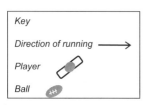

Key

Direction of running ———→

Player

Ball

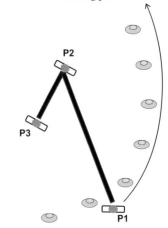

Figure 7.21(b) Full-back wingers into the line

POSITION – FULL-BACK AND WINGERS

DRILL | *DEFENDING A CHIP OR GRUBBER-KICK*

Aim

To develop explosive acceleration, deceleration, controlled turn, balance, co-ordination and re-acceleration to defend the opposition's chip or grubber-kick.

Area/equipment

Indoor or outdoor area – rugby ball, 2–3 kg hand weights and 3 cones set up in a straight line with 30 m between each cone.

Description

Player 1, the winger or full-back, stands on cone A holding the hand weights. Player 2 stands 20 m away on cone C with the ball in his hands. The drill commences with both players accelerating towards the centre cone B. When the distance between the players is approximately 1–2 m, player 2 chips or grubber-kicks the ball past player 1. Immediately, player 1 will decelerate, turn and re-accelerate to chase the ball. After the first 1–2 m of the re-acceleration phase, player 1 drops the weights and explodes towards the ball. Player 2 continues to put pressure on player 1 as he attempts to retrieve the ball.

Key teaching points

■ Maintain correct running form/mechanics
■ Use an explosive arm-drive during the deceleration and re-acceleration phases,
■ Do not sink into the hips
■ Drop the weights in a smooth, continuous running movement
■ Ensure that player 2 uses the correct kicking technique

Sets and reps

2 sets of 6 reps with a walk-back recovery between each rep and a 3-minute recovery between sets.

Variations/progressions

■ Introduce a support runner for the chip-kick to increase the pressure on player 1
■ Introduce an additional defender that player 1 can offload the ball to, in order to set up a counter-attack
■ When mastered, a combination of the above 2 drills will allow this drill to be continuous

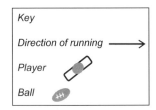

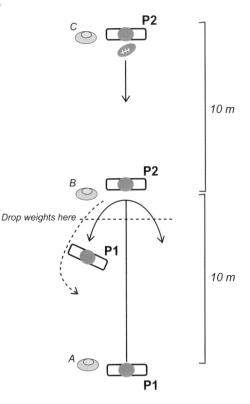

Figure 7.22 Defending a chip or grubber kick – full-back and wingers

POSITION – FULL-BACK

DRILL # EXPLOSIVE JUMP AND CATCH

Aim

To develop explosive vertical jumping ability and explosive multi-directional acceleration after the catch.

Area/equipment

Indoor or outdoor area – rugby balls, 1 Viper Belt and 6 cones set up as shown.

Description

Player 1 and player 2 are connected to each other by the Viper Belt. Player 1, the full-back, stands on the start cones A; player 2 stands on the centre of the flexi-cord, pinning it to the ground to provide vertical resistance to player 1. Player 3 stands just beyond the cones 1-4. The drill commences with player 3 throwing the ball into the air for player 1 to catch. As soon as the full-back has caught the ball, he accelerates to a cone nominated by player 3. Simultaneously player 2 takes his foot off the flexi-cord and remains stationary to provide resistance during the acceleration phase.

Key teaching points

- Full-back must use correct jumping mechanics
- Full-back must land on the balls of his feet
- Use short, explosive steps and arm-drive (even with the ball in the hands)
- Do not sink into hips – stay tall

Sets and reps

2 sets of 8 reps plus 2 contrast runs, with a walk-back recovery between each rep and a 3-minute recovery between sets.

Variations/progressions

- Introduce a clearance kick by the full-back
- Introduce opposition runners to apply pressure to the full-back.

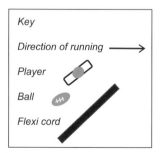

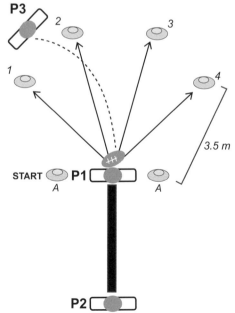

Figure 7.23 Full-back jump and catch

DRILL *RESISTED PLACE-KICKS*

Aim
To develop more power and greater distance from place-kicks.

Area/equipment
Large indoor or outdoor area – rugby balls, a punch/kick resistor and a kicking tee if required.

Description
The punch/kick resistor is fastened around the player's kicking foot and held by a second player from behind. The drill commences with the kicker placing the ball in the standard fashion and kicking the ball without any resistance. The resistor is then attached and the player performs 10 kicks without the ball. The resistor is taken off and then a ball is set up and kicked as normal.

Key teaching points
■ Ensure that the kicking mechanics/technique are correct
■ Player 2 must be sitting down to provide resistance and to restrict the kicker as little as possible

Sets and reps
1 set = 1 initial unresisted kick with the ball; 10 resisted kicks without the ball; 1 contrast (unresisted) kick with the ball.

Variations/progressions
■ Introduce resisted kicks with the ball
■ Use the same techniques for punt-kicks out of the hands

CHAPTER 8 WARM–DOWN AND RECOVERY

Due to the intense activity levels possible during the main part of the session, time should be given to gradually reduce the heart rate to near resting levels. This will help to:

- disperse lactic acid
- prevent blood pooling
- return the body systems to normal levels
- assist in recovery.

The structure of the warm-down will essentially be the reverse of the Dynamic Flex warm-up (*see* pp. 1–32) and will last for approximately 5 minutes, depending on the fitness level of the players. The warm-down begins with moderate Dynamic Flex movements: these will gradually become less intense and smaller in amplitude. The exercises should still focus on quality of movement (good mechanics).

Static stretches should then be incorporated following this stage of the session. Carry out stretches that mirror the movements that are being carried out in the warm-down.

DRILL HIGH KNEE-LIFT SKIP

Follow the instructions given on page 9.

Aim
To warm down the hips and buttocks gradually.

Sets and reps
2 × 20 metres, 1 forwards and 1 backwards.

Intensity
60% for the first 20 metres and 50% for the second 20 metres.

DRILL KNEE-ACROSS SKIP

Follow the instructions given on page 10.

Aim
To warm down the hip flexors gradually by lowering the intensity of the exercise.

Sets and reps
2 × 20 metres, 1 forwards and 1 backwards.

Intensity
50% for the first 20 metres and 40% for the second 20 metres.

DRILL WIDE SKIP

Follow the instructions given on page 7.

Aim
To warm down the hips and ankles.

Sets and reps
2 × 20 metres, 1 forwards and 1 backwards.

Intensity
40% for the first 20 metres and 30% for the second 20 metres.

DRILL CARIOCA

Follow the instructions given on page 22.

Aim
To warm down the hips and bring the core body temperature down.

Sets and reps
2 × 20 metres, 1 left leg leading and 1 right leg leading.

Intensity
30% for the first 20 metres and 20% for the second 20 metres.

DRILL WALKING HAMSTRING

Follow the instructions given on page 6.

Aim
To warm down the muscles of the lower leg and the ankle.

Sets and reps
2 × 20 metres, 1 forwards and 1 backwards.

Intensity
20% for the first 20 metres and 10% for the second 20 metres.

DRILL ANKLE FLICKS

Follow the instructions given on page 4.

Aim
To bring the heart rate down and to stretch the calves and ankles.

Sets and reps
2 × 20 metres, 1 forwards and 1 backwards.

Intensity
10% for the first 20 metres and then walking flicks for the second 20 metres.

DRILL | *HURDLE WALK*

Follow the instructions given on page 18.

Aim
To bring the heart rate down.

Sets and reps
2 × 20 metres, 1 forwards and 1 backwards.

Intensity
Walking.

DRILL | *SMALL SKIPS*

Follow the instructions given on page 20.

Aim
To stretch the backs of the thighs.

Sets and reps
2 × 20 metres, 1 forwards and 1 backwards.

Intensity
Walking.

DRILL | *LATISSIMUS DORSI STRETCH*

Aim
To stretch the muscles of the back.

Description
Standing in an upright position, link the hands together in front of the chest. Push the hands out, simultaneously arching the back forwards. Focus on slow, controlled breathing.

Key teaching points
- Do not force the arms out too far
- Focus on slow, controlled breathing

Sets and reps
Hold the stretch for approximately 10 seconds.

DRILL   QUADRICEPS STRETCH

Aim
To stretch and assist the recovery of the muscles at the front of the thigh.

Description
Stand on one leg, bring the heel of the other foot in towards the buttock. Using the hand of that side, hold the 'lace' area of that foot and squeeze it in to the buttock. Repeat on the opposite leg.

Key teaching points
- Try to keep the knees together
- Ensure that the support leg is slightly bent
- Press the hip forward
- Focus on slow, controlled breathing
- Do not force the stretch – just squeeze it in gently

Sets and reps
Hold the stretch for approximately 10 seconds on each leg.

Variation
The exercise can be performed while the player is lying down sideways on the floor.

DRILL   HAMSTRING STRETCH

Aim
To stretch and assist the recovery of the hamstrings at the backs of the thigh.

Description
Sit on the floor with one leg extended and the other leg bent. Bend forwards from the hips and reach down towards the foot.

Key teaching points
- Focus on slow, controlled breathing
- Bend forwards from the hips
- Keep the back straight
- Flex the foot to increase the stretch

Sets and reps
Hold the stretch for approximately 10 seconds on each leg.

DRILL ADDUCTORS STRETCH

Aim
To stretch and assist the recovery of the adductor muscles of the inner thigh.

Description
Standing with the legs apart, bend one knee, keeping the foot at an angle of 45°. The other leg should be straight. Repeat on the opposite leg.

Key teaching points
- Focus on slow, controlled breathing
- Do not force the stretch
- Keep the back straight
- Do not allow the knee of the bent leg to go beyond the toes

Sets and reps
Hold the stretch for approximately 10 seconds on each leg.

DRILL CALF STRETCH

Aim
To stretch and assist the recovery of the calf muscles.

Area/equipment
Indoors or outdoors.

Description
Standing with the legs apart, one in front of the other and both feet pointing forwards, transfer the weight to the knee of the front foot and then gently back. The back leg should be kept straight; it is this calf that will be stretched.

Key teaching points
- Focus on slow, controlled breathing
- Do not force the stretch
- Apply the weight slowly to the front foot

Sets and reps
Hold the stretch for approximately 10 seconds on each leg.

CHAPTER 9 THE SAQ RUGBY PROGRAMME

Modern rugby needs modern programmes which are periodised throughout the year and cater for individual positional needs. The most successful programmes are those that are varied, provide challenges, keep the players on their toes, accept individuality and are fun. Failing to provide a stimulating programme by providing too much of the 'same' is guaranteed to demotivate players and squads, resulting in compromised performances in both training and games.

Some simple rules

- start with Dynamic Flex

- complete explosive work and sprints early in the session, before any anaerobic work

- plan sessions so that an explosive session is followed by a preparation day

- progress from simple to complex drills

- don't restrict programmes to one-week periods; work with different blocks of 4–8–10–12 days

- teach one new skill a day

- plan rest and recovery periods well

- vary work-to-rest ratios

- build up strength before performing plyometrics

- keep each session short and sharp. Explanations and discussions should be conducted before and afterwards, not in activity time

- finish off each session with static (PNF) stretching

Pre-season training

For many years coaches and trainers have relied predominantly on the development of the aerobic energy system by utilising long, slow, steady-state runs from 5 miles to anything up to 8 miles. Research clearly shows that this type of running is unsuitable for rugby players – and in fact, is more likely to cause unnecessary overuse injuries and more importantly, slow players down.

Rugby is an intermittent, stop-start team-game of 80 minutes' duration, although the ball is actually only in play for an average of 30 minutes. Motion analysis in rugby indicates that most activity lasts for just a few seconds, with the average distance run per game-phase being approximately 15 metres. It is an explosive, dynamic game that utilises fast-twitch muscle fibres and therefore depends primarily on the anaerobic energy system. By training the anaerobic system a number of benefits are gained that impact on the overall level of rugby fitness. These are as follows:

- An increased ability to tolerate higher levels of lactate, which is a metabolic by-product that causes muscular fatigue if it is not dispersed

- An increase in aerobic power, which is the energy system that uses oxygen without 'turning off' the fast-twitch fibres – vital because it is these that enable players to perform explosive, multi-directional movements such as sprinting, jumping, tackling and diving.

- An improved recovery time – very important since it enables players to perform at a high intensity and to recover more quickly for the next activity.

SAQ CONTINUUM	DRILLS	SETS AND REPS	EQUIPMENT	PLAN	TIME
Dynamic Flex	All with ball	Up and back – each drill	Cones and balls	Work in pairs over a 20-metre split grid. Perform a Dynamic Flex drill over the first part of the grid, pick the ball up and perform a ball-skill up and back the second part of the grid. Return to the start by performing the Dynamic Flex drill backwards	18 mins
Mechanics	• Dead-leg run • Lateral step • Single-leg lead Introduce the ball at the end of the grid	1 set of 6 reps of each drill without the ball, and then 1 set of 6 reps with the ball	8 hurdles, cones and balls	Place the hurdles in a straight line with approximately 18 inches between each hurdle	10 mins
Innervation	• Single step • Lateral step • Hopscotch • Icky shuffle Introduce the ball in the middle for passing skills	1 set of 6 reps of each drill	4 single ladders, 4 cones and 2 balls	Place the ladders in a cross-formation, leaving a space in the middle of approximately 3 square metres	12 mins
Accumulation of potential	A skill circuit incorporating mechanics drills, fast-feet drills and the ball	1 set of 6 reps	12 cones, 2 ladders and 12 hurdles	Place the ladders, hurdles, cones in a circuit to provide the player with the opportunity to practise zig-zag, lateral and linear runs forwards and backwards, as well as jump, turn and acceleration mechanics. Incorporate the ball where possible	10 mins
Explosion	• Out and back (include a pass) • Lateral side-stepping • Jelly Ball hip-thrusts	1 set of 8 reps of each drill	Viper Belt, Side-Stepper, cones and balls	• Out-and-back – wearing a Viper Belt, work out and back out to 3 angled cones approximately 2.5 metres away • Zig-zag – wearing the Side-Steppers, work in a zig-zag pattern along the channel of cones that are around 2 metres apart • Wearing the Side-Steppers, jockey up and back along a 20-metre channel	18 mins
Expression of potential	• 'Circle the ball' • 'Robbing the nest'	1 game of approximately 3–4 minutes	Cones and a ball	Split the squad into 4 groups: set up 2 games which can be played simultaneously. After the game, swap the teams around	8 mins
Warm-down	Dynamic Flex and static stretching	Up and back – each drill and 10-second hold on static stretches	Cones	Work over a 20-metre grid for the Dynamic Flex, gradually decreasing the intensity of the drills	12 mins

Typical SAQ for rugby session

PRE–SEASON PROGRAMME: FULL–TIME

1 day	=	microcycle
14 days	=	mesocycle
42 days	=	macrocycle

	A.M.		P.M.	
MONDAY	**SAQ Session** Dynamic Flex Mechanics = 60%, power = 40% Ball and skill work Flexibility session	15–20 min 30 min 40 min 20 min	Dynamic Flex Interval running Stretching	15–20 min 30 min 15 min
TUESDAY	Weights Core stability work	15 min 20 min	Swimming Flexibility	30 min 20 min
WEDNESDAY	**SAQ Session** Dynamic Flex Mechanics = 40%, power = 60% Ball and skill work Interval runs	15–20 min 30 min 35 min 25 min	Rest	
THURSDAY	Weights Core stability work Flexibility	45 min 20 min 20 min	Dynamic Flex Wrestling Eye–hand co-ordination work Stretching	15–20 min 20 min 20 min 15 min
FRIDAY	**SAQ Session** Dynamic Flex Mechanics = 50%, power = 50% Stretching	15–20 min 45 min 15 min	Dynamic Flex Cross training ie basketball Interval work Stretching	15–20 min 20 min 30 min 15 min
SATURDAY	Weights Flexibility	45 min 20 min	Rest	
SUNDAY	Rest		Rest	

PRE-SEASON PROGRAMME: FULL-TIME contd.

	A.M.		**P.M.**	
MONDAY	**SAQ Session**		Weights	45 min
	Dynamic Flex	15–20 min	Core stability work	25 min
	Mechanics = 50%, power = 50%	30 min	Flexibility	20 min
	Ball and skill work	35 min		
	Interval runs	25 min		
	Stretching	15 min		
TUESDAY	Swimming pool work		Ball and skill work	60 min
	Dynamic Flex Pool Workout	35 min	Dynamic Flex	15–20 min
			Eye–hand co-ordination work	30 min
WEDNESDAY	Weights	45 min		
	Ball and skill work	45 min	Rest	
	Flexibility	20 min		
THURSDAY	**SAQ Session**		Dynamic Flex	15–20 min
	Dynamic Flex	15–20 min	Ball work	50 min
	Mechanics = 40%, power = 60%	35 min	Core stability work	25 min
	Interval work	30 min		
	Stretching	15 min		
FRIDAY	Weights	45 min	Rest	
	Flexibility	20 min		
SATURDAY	Dynamic Flex	15–20 min		
	Interval work	35 min	Rest	
	Swimming pool workout	30 min		
SUNDAY	Rest		Rest	

IN SEASON (with games on a Saturday)

	A.M.	P.M.		
MONDAY	Weights Core stability Flexibility	45 min 25 min 20 min	Dynamic Flex Team run Stretching	15–20 min 65 min 15 min
TUESDAY	Dynamic Flex SAQ Rugby-specific running	15–20 min 60 min	Rest	
WEDNESDAY	Weights Core stability Ball and skill work Stretching	45 min 25 min 45 min 15 min	Dynamic Flex SAQ Rugby Specific Skills position drills Stretching	15–20 min 60 min 15 min
THURSDAY	Swimming Flexibility	35 min 20 min	Rest and recovery	
FRIDAY	Dynamic Flex Team run Stretching	15–20 min 45 min 15 min	Rest and recovery	
SATURDAY	**Game**		Recovery immediately after the game	
SUNDAY	Rest and recovery		Rest and recovery	

NB: *rest* – feet up and do nothing; *recovery* – active, low intensity recovery, eg. swimming, walking, stretching, sauna, spa, massage.

Part–Time Programmes

Around the world, the majority of clubs that play rugby do so on a part-time basis. They normally train 2 or 3 times a week, depending on the level of rugby that they play. The SAQ Rugby Programme can make training interesting, challenging and also great fun.

You will be amazed how hard players work without realising it, and you will also get great results in all areas of their fitness. Do not fall into the trap of relying on steady-state runs. Interval running, SAQ rugby-specific drills and SAQ Rugby Circuits will help your players become fitter and faster.

PRE–SEASON PROGRAMME

14-DAY CYCLE

All sessions start with Dynamic Flex
(P) = Personal training session away from club

MONDAY	Weight-training programme and flexibility work (**P**)	
TUESDAY	Dynamic Flex	15 min
	SAQ Session	40 min
	Interval work:	
	Combination run	5 min (2 min)
	Rugby drills	5 min (2 min)
	Combination run	5 min (2 min)
	Rugby drills	5 min (2 min)
	Combination run	5 min (2 min)
	Rugby drills	5 min (2 min)
	Core development	
	Stretch	
WEDNESDAY	Active recovery, swimming, stretch, weights (**P**)	
THURSDAY	Dynamic Flex warm-up with ball	15 min
	SAQ Session	40 min
	Power work with Jelly Balls	
	Interval running	5 min (2 min)
	Rugby drills	5 min (2 min)
	Interval running	5 min (2 min)
	Rugby drills	5 min (2 min)
	Interval running	5 min (2 min)
	Rugby drills	5 min (3 min)
	Core development	
	Stretch	
FRIDAY	Weight-training programme	
	Stretch, swim, sauna (**P**)	
SATURDAY	Dynamic Flex warm-up with ball	15 min
	Power development (including recovery)	40 min (3 min)
	Rugby drills	40 min (3 min)
	Rugby-specific runs	20 min
	Stretch – swim	

NB: Time in brackets indicates recovery period before moving on to next element of session.

SUNDAY	Stretch, swim and rest	
MONDAY	Weight-training programme and flexibility (**P**)	
TUESDAY	Dynamic Flex with ball	15 min
	SAQ Session	40 min
	Interval work:	
	Combination run	5 min (2 min)
	Rugby drills	5 min (2 min)
	Combination run	5 min (2 min)
	Rugby drills	5 min (2 min)
	Combination run	5 min (2 min)
	Rugby drills	5 min (2 min)
	Core development	
	Stretch	
WEDNESDAY	Active recovery, swimming, stretch, weight-training programme (**P**)	
THURSDAY	Dynamic Flex with ball	15 min
	SAQ Session	40 min
	Power work with Jelly Balls for core development:	
	Interval running	5 min (2 min)
	Rugby drills	5 min (2 min)
	Interval running	5 min (2 min)
	Rugby drills	5 min (2 min)
	Interval running	5 min (2 min)
	Rugby drills	5 min (3 min)
	Stretch	
FRIDAY	Rest	
SATURDAY	Dynamic Flex with ball	15 min
	Power development (including recovery)	40 min (3 min)
	Rugby drills	40 min (2 min)
	Rugby-specific runs	20 min
	Stretch off – swim	
SUNDAY	Stretch, swim and rest	

NB: Repeat 14-day programme; reduce recovery times by 20 seconds in the first week and up to 30 seconds in the second week.

IN–SEASON – PART–TIME

MONDAY	Personal stretch, weight-training programme	50 min
TUESDAY	**SAQ Session** (including Dynamic Flex) Team and skill work Multi-sprints Stretching	40 min 35 min 20 min 15 min
WEDNESDAY	Personal weights, flexibility	50 min
THURSDAY	**SAQ Session** (including Dynamic Flex) Team run Stretching	35 min 60 min 15 min
FRIDAY	Stretching (**P**) and rest	
SATURDAY	**Game** and recovery	
SUNDAY	Swimming, recovery and rest	

References

Gleim, G.W. and McHugh, M.P. (1997), 'Flexibility and its effects on sports injury and performance', *Sports Medicine*, 24(5): pp. 289–299.

Pope, R. (1999), 'Skip the warm up', *New Scientist*, Vol. 164, No. 2214, (18/12/99): p. 23.

Smythe, R. (2000), 'Acts of agility', *Training and Conditioning*, Vol . V. No. 4, pp. 22–25.

Index of drills